I0554720

FACES OF INHUMANITY

NICHOLAS BARKER

HANGAR 1 PUBLISHING

1

W here shall I start? So much has happened since the events of the demonic presence that had plagued my aunt's manor. You see, it was these events that fueled a curiosity within myself and Mary. Originally, I must admit, I had a repulsion to such a haunting. Yet, in the time that slowly passed into the summer of 1853, I had many thoughts that dwelt upon the idea of demons and such entities. This later evolved into an obsession to understand the darkest reaches of the afterlife and spirits that rested in such places. So many questions that begged my mind for answers, but no answers that could be logically sound. I would venture so far as to say without the support of Percy and his family, I would not have succeeded in fighting off the demonic incursion.

Lessons relegated to an ancient tome that speaks of wondrous and frightful creatures of both good and evil, yet simply stories still. I shall state, however, this life that is now lived is nothing like any life that Mary and I could have possibly dreamed. It is the life that has brought fulfillment, I will admit. I also must question what would cause any sane man to give up a life of comfort and wealth within a career that could launch anyone further than he dreamed? What sort of man would continue to subject himself and his wife to a life of strife by dealing with the demons of others? I have assured myself, time and time again, that I am no longer logical or sound of mind. Yet I still freely choose the life I now live.

Mary has been supportive of any decision that I would have made for our

endeavors. Which, I suppose, shows that we are like-minded in our investigations. Yet she still has her desire to pursue a career by day. Though there have been sacrifices that she has willingly made. Words cannot describe how supportive and dependable Mary has been without respite. Yet again, I must focus on the forward progress of my endeavors. It all began once Mary and I had arrived in New York. It was a series of words spoken by a passenger waiting for the train to travel to the New York City platform. I believe it was a woman and her husband seated against the white timber outer wall of the ticket office. Her husband was reading a current edition of the local newspaper and didn't seem to regard his wife in the least. As Mary and I passed them, their faint words could be heard.

"According to our gazette, honey, Spiritualism may be a faster growing belief than we had thought before."

It was this statement that I could not have realized would pique my interest and come back to me in stalwart recollection. Like a pulsing screech in the inner recesses of my mind or a voice calling from deep within. I knew not what impact this event would have on me, though I often wondered if it was the same for Mary as well. Mary and I continued to stroll to the end of the building, mainly to stretch our legs after a long train ride to this platform. It felt good to take in the fresh air and see the sights that were now passing in the blink of an eye. Though, for me, these were the sights that I had witnessed on my fore mentioned journey. North Carolina had been a beauty for my eye to behold, but nothing like the sights that Mary and I were

absorbing now, however. Yet, in some ways, I preferred North Carolina; the natural beauty of the endless forests had been refreshing. Something as such was welcomed due to the reduction in population and a few large structures stole my eyes from the landscape's beauty. Although some cities are beautiful in themselves, even with such a stark contrast to forests and rolling hills.

Reaching the end of the platform, I could see the track leading my eyes into the distance. Each side of the track was lined with dense forest. All the vegetation was a beautiful, verdant color. Each leaf was a deep or bright green, with the darker leaves just behind the brighter leaves. This was a beautiful contrast that pleased my eyes as the trees stood tall and mighty against the sky. Their branches went in all directions and all met at a trunk that was larger than most trees that I had ever seen. While other branches hung down over the tracks in a thick curtain of grayish-brown and green. There was just enough space for a train to gently ride through the forest. Even above the trees, the sky was a deep blue, as if an ocean rolling above my head. Small and medium clouds hung gently in the breeze and seemed to glide slowly and gracefully across the sky while the day held a gentle heat with a light but immersive breeze.

Mary and I were relieved that the weather was stable and we were not met with a stiff wind. This would have made our travel unbearable, though I was sure that northern-bound tracks would see worse weather. As for now, the Southern New York-Yonkers platform was a welcomed sight. Mary had been relaying to me the notion of train travel being harmful to her usual lifestyle of being able to walk anywhere she liked. She had complained of her feeling bored, but most that her legs had become stiff, even despite our walking the length of the train. I had worried that this factor would deter Mary from riding trains in the future. What would follow would leave us with great difficulty when vacationing, but I did wonder about visiting Mary's family in the future. As I stood on the edge of the platform, my deep contemplation was broken by Mary's words. "What time is our departure, my love?" Mary asked, causing me to notice how refreshing her voice was to my ears.

I instantly awoke from my trance and could see Mary standing across from me on the other side of the platform. She was twisting her body back and forth slowly with her right leg tucked behind her left leg. She was gorgeous against the forest setting behind her and her dress, being a rosy color, was complemented by her shoulder-length brown hair. She had cocked her head slightly forward and was gazing at me with wondrous and gentle hazel eyes. A smile was gently placed below her eyes, her lips so soft and inviting were parted ever so slightly. Her whole appearance at this moment gave me pause. The woman before my eyes knew how to engage me in the most spectacular ways. Her catty nature, mixed with a voice that reminds me of a breeze whispering through a meadow, added to the experience. Each word gently arose to my ears and seemed to kiss my eardrum with the softest regard. She had the voice of an angel who had never risen to heaven.

"Yes, my dear," I replied. "Our departure is promptly at 2 PM."

Mary then asked, "And our time now?"

I looked to my left and up slightly to the clock that hung on the side post of the ticket-box office, each hand moving calculatedly in a race around an endless track of numbers.

"Currently, I can see 1:35 PM, my love," I replied.

Mary seemed disturbed by this answer as she stared from the platform to the tracks below.

"I feel that we have been at this station for hours. Could time pass any slower?" Mary looked up to meet my eyes as she finished this statement.

We both chuckled, yet we seemed to both be thinking the same thing. If only our train had not split off from our schedule to deliver cargo to Buffalo, New York. Though it seems to be a waste as New York City is along the way. I do hope that the next train is scheduled to travel to the great city, otherwise, there will be more delay.

"I am sorry, my dear," I stated. "I have not dealt with delays before as most of the trips that I have taken ensured my train traveling directly to New York City."

Mary asked, "Do you think that something could have gone wrong?"

I replied, "I doubt it, my wife. If there had been a change in the train schedules, then we would've been informed when we arrived. I would say that this platform is having a delay with the engine being loaded with freight. Then the train arrives at our location promptly but partially loaded with freight from another area. I suspect this would speed freight delivery to places like Buffalo."

Mary looked down the platform that we stood upon and I could see her mind turning my statements over and over. At some point, her thoughts had concluded.

"Benjamin, my love, how is it that you are so easily capable of making new possibilities available to me? Never have I met a man who has pushed me to consider all possibilities."

While Mary spoke these words, she closed the distance and placed her hands on my chest. She leaned in and kissed me so passionately that I couldn't help but feel a rush of stimulation slowly creep up from my chest and rise to the crown of my head.

Though I could not see my face, I knew that I was smiling ear to ear, but try as I might, I couldn't stop my emotions from showing. Not that I would wish to be stony or cold to anyone. I just think of myself as a more reserved person and Mary had come into my life, I believed, to change everything.

"My wife, I am more than a mere man, yet I have come down to inspire you in flesh form," I stated with a large smile.

Mary nodded with a very playful smile on her face as I took her hand and we began strolling slowly down the platform to find a seat. The other passengers had crowded around the ticket box, with some passengers seated on the far side of the platform as we had. Yet each group seemed to form little herds and only associated with others if approached. Otherwise, everyone else seemed extremely inviting. Group after group of passengers passed by as we strolled as swiftly and gracefully as possible, moving through each group of passengers only when no other option presented itself.

Everyone seemed to be dressed to impress others in their expensive dresses flowing in the breeze, fine suits made of different silks, and each passenger wore a hat of some sort. From taller stove-pipe hats to a shorter bowler style, some hats with wider brims and some with more narrow brims but all colors of fabric were represented. After we had passed the last group of passengers closest to the ticket office, we beheld an empty seat. No one seemed to be focused on finding a seat other than us, so we helped ourselves. Mary turned and began taking her seat beside me gracefully, sweeping her dress out and under her legs as she then took her seat.

It was then that an amusing thought crossed my mind and I turned my head toward where Mary was seated with a twisted half smile forming on my face.

"Mary, my dear, do you find it difficult to sit down in a beautiful dress such as yours?" I asked, still smiling with a devious look.

She replied without hesitation, "I do. I think any woman would since we are forbidden in a lot of cases from voicing any opinion on the matter."

I smiled wider, "Perhaps you could try pants for a change."

Without question, Mary replied, "I would love to, Benjamin, but as I have said, it wouldn't be proper!"

It was at this point that the realization set in about what I was trying to accomplish.

"Benjamin Price! I do not think your sick taunts are humorous! I forbid you from trapping me with your words again! Otherwise, you shall find yourself quite seldom!" With these words, Mary turned her head away and refused to speak. I knew better than to be loud with any laughter, so I chuckled as quietly as I could to myself.

"I can hear you giggling like a schoolboy, Benjamin! I suppose you are rather pleased with yourself! Do you value my desires and passions so minimally?"

I gazed at Mary with blank eyes and a full smile.

"It isn't that that I hold no value for your desires and certainly not your passions, my wife. I sometimes long to jest with you in my way, but it isn't to make you feel like someone less just to make you laugh."

Mary stared into my eyes with a look of deep annoyance. She replied with a blank face, "Then, if you wish to amuse me, maybe you should give a dress a try. That would be the only way that something like this would amuse me." Mary giggled about this thought for a moment, as did I.

The time now seemed to pass slowly, extremely slow, in fact, as

Mary and I continued to sit. We talked about the events of the day, and I had even begun to explain the finer points of life within the city. I thought that it would be exceptionally helpful because Mary had never resided in such a place. Larger populations seemed to shock anyone when they first arrived in New York City, and I wished to ensure that Mary would have the best and strongest chance of settling into a life in the grand city. So, in time, I had begun to explain everything that I could about this lifestyle, to which Mary seemed the utmost eager to learn all that she could.

I was astonished at her ability to receive information so readily that it seemed she gave no resistance. She also didn't offer anything in the way of resistance to the content of my message to her either. I supposed that she saw my words as no threat to her, her passions, or her intelligence. Instead, she absorbed everything that I had to say; her eyes did not once drift from my gaze, even when covering the subject of different groups that called the city home. Many failed to understand the city was home to many that the world had forgotten. Those that did not belong elsewhere or were the type of people that abandoned their countries of origin for life, liberty, and the pursuit of happiness. Each had come to claim one thing; freedom.

Above all else, freedom was able to be obtained on the shores of New York, though others sought to destroy this. Anarchists, thieves, and politicians are all seeking to take freedom from all who obtain it. People would not be oppressed so easily, however, as I believed in my heart that even New Yorkers wouldn't give up their freedoms. No one could begin to understand the vastness of the culture of New York City as people wondered about it at any hour that they wished. Many a late evening out courting their future brides, still others seeking relaxation with spirits and strolls about the parks. Most people out by day strolling the streets, heading to work or seeking the day's work independently and churches witnessing to their flock.

Anyone could even find commerce on any street at most hours of the day.

Especially in the high towns, which were areas known for patrons with unlimited wealth and reach. Workers pass in the streets with carts full of materials, building the city from ground to sky. Forming the framework of modern society and crafting such impressive structures or adding to existing ones. Seldom did this form of labor cease as workmen were in short supply and building projects were far too numerous.

This was the way of an ever-expanding city; this and other factors would drive anyone mad, especially when many have no point of reference. Nowhere in the world could there be a life such as this and I have even heard from colleagues within the great cities of London, Paris, and even Berlin; yet all are flabbergasted by the depth of American ingenuity. This was the underlying factor of immense awe that many felt when traveling to New York City. Mary absorbed the endless amount of information that I could share and she did not look away or ask any questions. No, she just sat listening to my words with the most eager expression, yet I could see that Mary had accepted that her life was going to change forever.

In my younger days, I journeyed to the city with certain expectations. Many of these expectations gave me pause and seemed to disappoint me; this was only because I couldn't fathom the depth of life within New York City. Yet nothing could have been more interesting and instead of further study, I was met with an opportunity to start work immediately. Also, the chance to further my career without needing to study as hard as others. Moving into the city seemed to launch my life in a much more positive direction. I seemed to have success being presented to me in every direction that I would turn.

This was the world that I had understood would be best for my wife and children. Farm life was not a life that Mary had desired. Perhaps she didn't know what she truly wanted for her life, but she knew her life was not meant to include farming. The day continued to pass rather slowly, but after some time, Mary and I had begun to ponder if the train would ever arrive. Just as this thought had passed my lips and Mary agreed, the train whistle could be heard. There was a faint screeching further down the track as everyone began moving into lines and awaiting the train to open its doors. Many tucked their kids close to them and began checking their luggage, while others seemed to not pay the train any mind. It was as if these passengers were locked in an eternal gossip, left to stand on the platform in segregation.

Mary and I grasped our luggage from the middle of the platform and began to wait as well, but something still drew my gaze to the still conversing passengers. Yet I refused to turn my head and look as if I did not know what force wished me to turn my attention to these passengers, but the attraction grew stronger. Instead, I kept my gaze upon Mary and tried with all that I had in me to hear her words, but I could hear nothing. It was as if I had fallen into a pool of water which was distorting all sound from my hearing while my sight had become a blur. I felt as though someone was staring right through me from behind and this feeling continued until the train had pulled into position.

At this moment, I began to follow Mary, but everything slowed to a crawl; it was as if I could hear voices in my mind. They drowned out all other sounds as if nothing else could be heard above the roar of numerous voices. Some were laughing and some were simply talking about many different things, but almost as if different conversations were being carried on at the same time. I could not pinpoint any one conversation or word while this feeling rose until I couldn't resist it any longer. I began turning my head in the direction of the conversing passengers and noticed they were now huddled together as if sharing a secret. I approached the train door at an angle that gave me a perfect view of this mass of passengers. Just as I had been able to focus on each member of this group, they stopped what they were doing.

Their heads snapped up and then turned to look back at me with the most sinister grin on their faces which left me alarmed but curious. I couldn't look away, but it was more as if I could not turn my head rather than not wanting to turn my head. I met eyes with the closest male passenger, who maintained his startling grin and nodded his head toward me slowly while they all began to fade. They vanished before my very eyes, leaving me with the desire to continue to watch until they had completely faded. It was at this time I had reached the train, but time was still passing slowly as I looked up to meet Mary's gaze. She was already most of the way up the steps of the passenger car as time began to resume its normal flow in a blur of motion.

"Did you spy that group, dear?" I asked.

Mary gazed into my eyes with a most puzzled look on her face. "I witnessed nothing." She replied.

I turned and pointed to where the huddle of passengers had stood.

She replied, "What, my love?"

I remarked cautiously, "Other passengers were standing right there. They vanished before my very eyes."

Before Mary could reply, the conductor asked to see our tickets. As I met his eyes and slowly reached into my pocket, I was startled to see anyone at this moment. I had a feeling that anyone besides myself, including Mary, was an illusion. Drifting into nothingness as if life itself were going to fade to reveal itself to be a lie. My senses could not be trusted at all, and I felt as if I were expecting the worst from anything and everything I beheld. *Could it be that life was not real? Was there some grand illusion waiting to reveal itself? Should I trust myself to know what is real and what is fake?* There seemed to be no way to test for any illusions, but I had an automatic knowing that I wouldn't be met with success if I began testing life itself.

I reached into the deepest depths of my right pocket only to grasp a wafer-thin piece of paper. It was almost as if I had grasped a fake ticket, but I knew that I had purchased my tickets shortly after we had arrived. I pulled the tickets from my pocket and gave them to the conductor, who took them from my hand with a cautious motion. As he inspected my ticket, he seemed to be puzzled at the expression of questioning on my face, as if he knew that I was questioning reality

itself. Perhaps he was doing the same, or he saw the same thing and he wanted confirmation as I had. After a moment, however, he punched both tickets and said, "Come with me, sir, madam.".

He then briefly met my gaze, then Mary's and turned to lead us into the passenger car. We walked through the passenger car, moving past row after row of seats. Most were filled with passengers, but each seemed to celebrate the train's arrival. Luggage had been tucked under the seats neatly and nothing seemed out of place. We continued to travel forward through the car and eventually reached the center of the car. Rows of windows flanked us on each side and the whole car was covered in a lavish deep blue and gold carpet. The windows to our left were that of a private compartment within the train car, and to our right, the windows allowed access to the outside world. The walls were paneled with what looked like finely carved mahogany, with each window holding the crest of the train company carved into the panel beneath it.

About halfway down the corridor, the conductor had come to a stop and stood in the corridor, holding out his right hand. He held his hand out to guide us into the compartment politely.

"This is your compartment, sir, madam. Enjoy your trip and let us know if you require anything," he said.

Mary and I entered the compartment and immediately began settling in for the long journey. I then noticed that someone had set the table and placed refreshments on the side of the table closest to the window. Mary and I sat facing each other whilst admiring the world through our window. The world seemed to stand still from here as nothing moved and no one stood waiting on the platform. I could barely see the place where I had witnessed the other passengers vanish, but now it seemed normal, as if nothing had happened just moments before.

The feelings of confusion and alarm had now passed, yet I could picture the huddle of passengers staring at me. Their faces were accented by the creepiest smile I have ever witnessed from another human. Though I wouldn't venture to classify anyone there as a human, I still couldn't shake the thought that each one was still in their respective place. It seemed that my mind wished to simply think of these people as invisible, yet I had an intense feeling that no one in that wretched group had existed in the flesh for some time. I continued to stare outside for a few more moments, that is until I heard Mary's voice, "Are you all right, my love?".

Her words took some time to rouse me from my trance, but after a couple of minutes, I turned to see her leaning in the direction of the window as if trying to get in front of my eyes to block my vision or see what had my attention so strongly.

"Benjamin?" She queried.

I met her eyes with mine and replied, "Yes, my love?".

Mary seemed extremely concerned. "You are a ghostly white, my dear. Is everything okay?".

I nodded my head forward. "Yes. Everything is perfectly fine. I am just thinking."

Mary began making herself tea from the hot water on the table, "Is this about the people that you saw outside?".

I began to shake my head no but stopped suddenly, "No...I mean...Yes. Everything happened so quickly yet slowly at the same time."

Mary looked on intently, "I am sorry, dear. I don't mean to alarm you. I am probably just weary from so much travel." I said calmly.

Mary thought for a moment. "Perhaps you should lie down for a moment in your seat.".

I had no intention of resting, though I felt that I should do as Mary suggested and then decided that I couldn't ignore her input. After all, we still had several hours

before we were to reach the train station in the city. I followed Mary's suggestion and began preparing my seat to be a makeshift bed. Then I reached into the cabinets above me and pulled down some blankets. Mary scooted out of her seat and pulled the shades closed on the doors to the cabin. I stood beside my seat and removed my jacket from over my vest, then removed my pocket watch from its resting place in my vest pocket and placed it on the table.

I unhooked the clip on the other end and laid the chain in a coil on the table. In what seemed like an instant, I was laying on my side in my seat and covering myself with the blankets that I had procured from the cabinets overhead. Mary sat silently in her seat. I could feel that she was concerned but didn't wish to push a confession from me. I slowly began to drift from consciousness as the world faded from my eyes then I saw only blackness. I began to feel as though I was drifting from the place where my body was located, as if being pulled into a void.

The feeling was different now, however, as it was not only my physical body being pulled but another portion of my person that had separated. My mind had become disturbed, but I could no longer stop myself at all in my vision unless this could be a dream. I could not wake myself nor force my body to move, almost as if I had been disconnected from my flesh and bone. Being forever cast adrift from myself. The world became darkness that I could not escape, and I was being pulled deeper into the void of this realm. My body lingered in the space of the living and remained in the seat on the train. My soul was drifting further away from this world and into nothingness. This feeling was stranger than I had ever known as it was not a feeling or knowing that connected me to any earthly realm. Yet a faint understanding of what was and what might be as well as what was to come. There was no worry, no pain, no strife, just emptiness, and I was alarmed at these new sensations, but there was nothing that could stop this now.

I opened my mouth to scream for Mary, but no sound could be heard as this void stifled every sound or feeling and grew larger as my mind drifted further away. I wanted to wake up from this world and escape this horror, but there was nothing that I could control or change. It was then that I looked into the void and saw bright stars and different colors, as if I had been pulled from the Earth completely. I was not traveling at any increasing rate yet simply drifting like a boat with no oars on a gentle pond. I looked back toward my body and began reaching

outward and calling out for Mary. There was no sound and no way that I could connect with this world. I then felt the world slip from my grasp until there was no warmth, no light, only the darkness that pulled me further inward. I turned and began to tumble toward the furthest point of this realm, and I imagined that this is what it would be like to fall from the sky.

Even with all that was happening, nothing here felt real in the slightest, as I had been cast into an endless sea without anything to save me. Now that sea had changed to falling toward oblivion. I could feel panic and fear that seemed to instantly wash over me but seemed to not have a source either within or without. I grasped forward and reached as far as I could, but there was nothing solid to grasp or stop myself from drifting further. I looked back toward the world that I had seemingly fallen from originally. Not even a memory of what the world was or how it had left me behind.

I was alone and with no way back from this endless darkness, yet this feeling of fear began to grow more and more until I became overcome with this same fear. I looked down again and began to see it, the face from Caroline's manor. It was rushing toward me as quickly as it could with teeth bared and malice in its burning eyes. I was struck with terror now that gripped my heart and seemed to invade my very soul. I felt as if I were being devoured by this evil and entertained that I was surely dreaming as this entity had been defeated by myself. I screamed as I rushed headlong into the void that was this beast's mouth and plummeted into a sea of darkness. I then began to be pulled under the surface of this murky water and I could not stop the inevitable immersion of myself. What seemed to be the embodiment of terror and misery in liquid form. The battle between myself and whatever force continued to pull at my feet was now lost and I felt myself submerge in this emotion.

2

I awoke from a deep slumber in the train compartment only to hear the door open. I looked to my right to see Mary carrying water for both of us. I wasn't sure what time it was nor how much time had passed since I fell asleep.

"My love, I brought you water. This train is beautiful and enchanting." Mary said.

I simply nodded in acknowledgment as Mary handed me a glass of water while she settled comfortably into her seat. I was thankful that she was enjoying our travel rather than allowing herself to be impatient again as we moved through the countryside.

"What is the time, my love?" I asked.

Mary placed her glass of water on the table and said, "I believe the time is three in the afternoon.".

I smiled at her and replied, "Thank you, dear. How are you enjoying our journey so far?".

Mary thought for a moment.

"I am greatly enjoying our trip. The country here is beautiful! I have never sighted rolling hills covered in green", she said.

I could see her face reflecting her love for the sights as the train hurdled down the track.

Mary was a beautiful but practical woman with hopes and dreams but often kept herself in line with reality through those dreams. Though lately, it seemed that I had kept her more grounded in her beliefs and reality. She was the love of my life and there was nothing more that could stop me from desiring the best for her in our new life.

I sat back in my seat and took in a deep breath, only to exhale what felt like tension in a tangible form. The ordeal that had played out in my dreams had profoundly scarred my mind. It was something that I could not stray from within these following moments. Mary had no idea that I had struggled as I did since fighting for our lives against such a twisted being. I was sure now that Mary could understand. *Would she be able to bring herself to face such a thing?* Could it be that my understanding of her as a beautiful and frail being blinded me to an inner strength against such horrible things in life? I did not wish to bring her reality crashing down around her as had mine such a short time ago.

Though I knew that I would have to do so at some point in the future.

"My love, did you rest well?" Mary asked.

I was hesitant to answer but eventually said, "I did, my love. Though I feel that my dreams were more vivid than usual, I was not able to remember the contents upon waking.".

I allowed a nervous smile to cover my face as I held my tongue to cover my true feelings within that moment. Mary didn't seem to notice that I had locked myself away from her or if she did then she certainly didn't show it.

I did what I could to gather myself before finally saying,

"My love. I feel that I need to get some air, I will be back shortly. Rest and ready yourself for an adventure once we arrive in New York City.".

I then kissed Mary's forehead and moved cautiously through the door to the compartment and down the hall of the car. The only thought in my mind was to reach the smoking compartment and open a window to the rushing summer air outside. As swiftly as I could, I walked through two cars and into the smoking car. The smell of the car itself was of earthy and sweet tones of tobacco that moved through the air. Some smoked a pipe while others puffed on a cigar. I was not of such class to partake of cigars, rather, I enjoyed my pipe as much as I could. I produced my churchwarden from an inner coat pocket within my jacket. I then began packing my pipe with a pinch of tobacco. Following this, I reached into the box on the table to my left and produced a match to light my pipe. Within a few puffs, I was smoking a rather smooth tobacco from the stem of my pipe and could feel the relaxation of mind and body taking hold. I gently motioned to the waiter until he had begun to approach my table.

"Good sir, could I trouble you to lower my window to an appropriate and calming level?" I asked.

"Yes, sir. Could I bring you a drink?" The waiter asked.

"I would indeed enjoy a whiskey to sip. Thank you, sir."

The attendant lowered my window quickly only to move away from my seat to begin making a drink. I was left a few moments to enjoy the wind that entered the window and caressed my face. Nothing could match the feeling of such a mixture of sensations, between the delicious fragrances of tobacco and the fresh summer air. *Had I truly witnessed an event of such horrible proportions or was this simply something with which my mind is trying to come to grips?*

I could not be certain by any measure and no one seemed to notice that I had even entered the car or sat in my seat. I did not wish to be rude by slowly moving my eyes around the car and taking in the habits of each person that sat in the train car. It was sure to be embarrassing for anyone to meet my gaze, even for just a moment. It was then that I realized this was nothing more than the fears that seemed to take me over, but I still didn't wish to be deemed odd either.

I would not wish for my new wife to be bored without her husband around to tend to her needs. This was the way of thinking that seemed novel in a time such as this though who was I but a novel man. I longed to be with Mary even as I had just left her within our compartment. I was smitten by her and the way that she lived with and loved me. She held an animal attraction that enticed my most basic urges.

Though reality did collide within my mind as I gazed down to see the bowl of my pipe was still mostly full and there would be no issue leaving the car with a mostly full pipe in my pocket. That was simply not something that I wished to do at this moment. It was then that I had come to realize that the dreams that seemed to fill my vision in my sleep were nothing more than signaling that I had lost my grip on reality and had fallen into deep darkness. This demon had called to me in my dreams and tried to drag me into this realm of shadows once again. These dreams were something that I would have to refuse and resist at all costs. Perhaps it was also true that my time within that realm had touched my mind. This would cause me to leave a piece of myself there or allow a piece of the shadows to take my mind in my dreams.

In either case, I was sitting in a smoking car gazing at a man who gazed back and he continued to stare even if I looked away, which made me feel unusual. He seemed to have a fire to his gaze that locked me within that moment. At first, it was the feeling that someone had taken notice of me but then moved quickly to me noticing this man noticing me. Then after many moments of trying to look somewhere else, I could not avoid the fact that he was staring at me.

At this moment, I did what any rational person would do and stared back continuously. If this man was not unnerved by this, then something was certainly playing out of which I did not desire to be part. I certainly hoped that no one else would notice us staring at each other, nor did I wish for this man to approach or try to contact me, but at this point, I was content and somewhat amused to stare at him as well.

I puffed away on my pipe for a few more moments and continued staring at this man until the waiter approached and silently slid a message to me at my table. It appeared that this was the preferred method for this man to contact me as I slid the note toward me and read every word:

Do not take notice of the darkness that follows you. Do not acknowledge or speak of this evil that lingers around you, sir. I will contact you once the time is right.

-Edgar

I was alarmed by these words that had been elegantly scrawled on such a small piece of paper. This man had undoubtedly been following me for some time or had even been tasked with following me around. Nothing could describe my sense of paranoia at this moment. I could do nothing when I looked toward where this man was just sitting and noticed that he had left. The door didn't seem disturbed, nor did it seem that he was even real, as he seemed to be a hallucination. I considered the option that I could be asleep as well and this was nothing more than a dream that seemed all too real. I could not understand how I would not know that I was asleep, yet this certainly seemed like a good possibility.

Much to my surprise, no one else in the room seemed to notice this gentleman who had glared so intently in my direction. This was not surprising from most of the men in the room, but there were two that surely would have noticed. Even as they seemed to be smoking and looking about the room as well. Nothing in my mind could make sense of this situation as if this person was a figment of my imagination. *How would I have received this tangible note?* Something had obfuscated my mind and I considered the possibility that Mary might have been visited by this individual as well. Perhaps she may have witnessed this man also. This thought gave me the drive to stamp out the lit tobacco within my pipe and move quickly out of the smoking car. I must reach the compartment in which Mary would be resting.

Other passengers seemed to be up and moving around much more now as we neared New York City. I could not let this stop me, however, as my mind raced with the idea that Mary would need me if someone had infiltrated our compartment. My feet moved at a very brisk pace as I raced down the isles in the sitting car. I felt as if nothing could have ended my momentum without being removed from my path or being swept asunder. I rounded the edge of the door to the compartment and quickly opened it to see Mary sitting quietly and drinking her tea. It seemed as if nothing had changed since my departure from the smoking car.

"I am back, my love. Did you see a man rushing by our compart-ment?" I asked

confidently.

Mary looked up at me as if she had barely noticed that I had left for any amount of time.

"No, dear. I did not see anyone move past the window since you left." Mary replied.

Mary gazed into my eyes with a slight smile and big doe-eyes that simply made her irresistible. I then came to my senses and saw that we weren't alone and beyond that, we were close to our destination. Though it would be a short coach ride to our neighborhood, I could not count this as it was no more than an hour until we would be in our comfortable home. I moved to the seat opposite Mary and slid into a comfortable position at the table. I was pleased, above all, that Mary was safe and the stranger had not accosted her by any means. In fact, Mary seemed to be completely calm as she sat looking out the window at the trees going by in rapid succession.

Nothing could have been a better sight while sipping tea appar-ently, as Mary's eyes seemed glued to the window and she seemed to barely notice me looking upon her. Happiness was all that I desired for Mary in this new life that I had begun to introduce to her. Mary needed a world in which she could grow and change in the ways of a woman and a capable woman at that. After all, I could not be satisfied with a woman who clung to me at every turn and could not handle business on her own. Just as I finished these thoughts, the train conductors were moving throughout the train giving the final call of arrival. Mary instantly turned her head toward the door and then back to me.

"I cannot wait to see the city, Benjamin. This is so exciting!" Mary exclaimed.

She still held a firm smile on her face that was as genuine as a child eagerly awaiting the Christmas Season. The most concerning thing that hung in my mind was Mary and I arriving to our new home and beginning the process of settling into a new life with my new wife. The secondary concern was that of investigating this individual who seemed so mysterious. I could not count on the option that he was any threat to me *or* my new family, but it was odd. Though I was not someone to simply fear for my life or that of Mary without evidence. Nothing could have suggested that this person could be a threat especially given that this man had never even approached me. I am interested mainly in understanding the cause of a strange and focused mad following me. I still held curiosity about the information that he wished to share with me.

Perhaps I have done something that would cause an organization to be interested in myself or my actions and I knew that I would not be able to contain my interest unless I were able to forego all thoughts pertaining to this subject. Instead, I willed myself to carry our bags from the compartment in the train car onto the platform. I was also fortunate that I could see the coach driver standing not far away from the platform. I could no longer worry about the manner with which I would move our luggage from the platform. I did intend to assist the driver in any case as I could not wish to break the back of the driver. His was a valuable service to our society and came with harder work than would be thought.

Mary simply looked about at all of the other passengers moving around the platform and collecting luggage as if fleeing some disaster. We both approached the coach driver and introduced ourselves. He immediately tipped his hat to Mary and moved toward the luggage. I assisted the driver as best I could and then helped Mary into the coach. The driver then took his place on the coach seat as I climbed inside and prepared for our short journey to our new home. All around the train platform, people moved about with haste as others arrived to board the next line of trains from the city to other areas. The grounds were beautiful with trees and flowers that only reflected the beauty of this great city to all those who would arrive.

I was not sure if Mary would notice the beauty of the city or if she would be taken aback by all of the new sites and smells that wafted about the air. It was all too easy to not take everything in with a city this size unless you were a resident of said city for some time. Certainly, this city could not be seen in just one visit with such an immense and sprawling development. The driver and I were unfazed by all the enormous buildings and city centers containing shops and eateries of all kinds. Wealth flowed through the streets of this city as nowhere else in the world and nothing could cement this more than passing the first promenade on our right only to turn down our street. We could see shops lined up on both sides of the streets with people conducting business.

Mary was being tortured by all the sights that she was not able to experience simply riding along in a coach. She was pulled in by the immensity of the city and the ability to be provided anything that she longed to have and some things that she was not aware she needed. These were the amenities that I missed so dearly after traveling to North Carolina and not being able to receive all the benefits of living in what seemed to be the largest trading hub in the world. Anything that the heart desired was a short walk from our home to one of the many shops in our community. The shopkeepers were always the most helpful and friendly as they could only thrive by those who wished to purchase goods. Trade was all around us now and it was a glorious showing of all that Capitalism could offer.

The coach rolled down the street at a mostly even pace but would bounce slightly when hitting a rut in the road. Nothing was more uncomfortable than traveling through a forest with only dirt roads, however. Yet there was less enchantment about the city than in the rural forests of North Carolina. I would say that the beauty was about the same, but nothing could compare to the comfort of living within the city, which made all the difference. A few more moments passed as we stopped on the street just in front of our home. I was one of the lucky men who could call this whole home theirs rather than living within a boarding house or other multi-family dwelling. As the thought of moving into this home and leaving the apartment life behind entered my mind, I could see that Mary was now gazing up at the structure with delight and amazement. Surely she was pleased with our new home rather than disgusted, but only time would tell.

"Welcome to our home, dear!" I said emphatically.

Mary gave no response to what I had just said and instead just nodded while still gazing up in amazement from the window of the coach at the slightly weathered, brick home. She was as speechless as I had hoped that she would be at this moment.

"I am sorry, Benjamin. Did you say something?" Mary asked innocently.

She smiled slightly in anticipation of what I would say next.

"That is quite all right my love. I was saying that this is our home and I am hoping that you will enjoy living here," I replied.

"This is the most beautiful home I have ever laid my eyes upon, my love. You are truly a man of taste!" She added.

"Thank you, dear. I am glad that you like our home. Now I will help our driver pull our luggage from the top of the coach." I finished.

Mary simply nodded as I moved out of the door and into the street. It didn't take long to move to the other side of the coach and begin catching our luggage as it is being handed down to me. I moved as quickly as I could until all the luggage was laying on the ground all around me. I then opened the door for Mary and allowed her and her dress to clear the doorway of the coach before I closed it behind her. Mary and I walked to the door while I produced the key from my pocket and prepared the key to unlock the front door. I then assisted Mary as she walked up the steps from the street to the actual door. With a swift clicking of the lock after injecting the key into the keyhole and turning it slowly to the right.

The lock was that of a heavy master lock that I had installed upon purchasing the home as I did not wish to give a criminal any idea of breaking into my home. Though, for the rest of the criminal ilk, I kept a revolver loaded and on my person as I went to and from work. This was not due to mistrust of others, but I did not wish to be unprepared in any circumstance. I pushed the heavy door open swiftly and motioned for Mary to enter the home and to make herself comfortable out of the summer heat. After such, I moved down to the street again to pay the driver and retrieve our luggage quickly. I approached the coach and said,

"I thank you for your help, sir. This would not have been easy to make it home with all of our luggage."

The driver nodded and replied, "It was my pleasure, sir. Would you like me to assist you in bringing the luggage inside the home?"

I shook my head and handed the driver a plentiful tip. "That won't be necessary sir, I will take care of it."

The driver's eyes grew very large as he saw the tip in my hand, hesitant to take it. Eventually, he did, however, and bowed in a gracious motion then placed the tip into his pocket. He then insisted that he help me bring the luggage into the home. I was not going to allow this, but I did wish him a happy day and sent him on his way. He snapped the reins on his horse and rode gently down the street and out of sight. After that, I began moving the luggage into the home and placed them in the doorway. Once this was finished it was a simple budging of the door to close it. Mary had begun settling into our new home here in the city as quickly as she could. I also shared the excitement that Mary displayed as I had never lived within a home in my adult life.

I had always lived just down the street from the bank where I worked in a medium-sized apartment above an old store, but that all changed when I purchased this home, just before leaving for North Carolina. A coworker at the bank had wished to sell the home due to a relative moving outside the city, causing them to liquidate the home quickly. I felt compelled to take the opportunity and purchased the home with a rather large down payment. Now I find myself wishing to share a life with Mary who surely would not be content living above a crowded and loud shop. Yet, I did have to question whether this was just my embarrassment for such a meager life or a true desire to give Mary more than a cramped space with nothing more than one window.

I moved from the entryway of the home toward the stairs that led up to the

second level. Immediately an odd feeling fell upon me and I

could not catch my breath. It was that same feeling of dread that I felt in North Carolina, but I was not sure how it could be here in this home. I tried to look about the area while this weight hung from my heart and attempted to drag me into despair. I could not see any darkness or shadow that seemed to herald the beast that I had once faced. Still, I could not discount the fact that this thing had followed me here, but I could not begin to understand how. Could it be that such evil could attach itself to Mary or me and bring itself from such a long way? I could not take any chances and spoil Mary's perception of our new life. I would not allow this to corrupt my wife and her virtues.

I moved with a cautious grace toward the upper level of the home on the darkened oak stairs which creaked with every step that I took. I felt that I was working toward a goal that I really did not wish to have in my life. It was as if I was hesitant to even investigate this situation rather than ignoring everything and trying to live in blissful ignorance. I could not be sure, but I thought that my heart was being pulled into my stomach and I would not be able to recover from this dread that was heavy upon my chest. Each step toward the final landing was ever more painful as I could feel the dread intensify. After what seemed like an eternity, I finally reached the doorway to the guest bedroom. The door had been opened and seemed to be moving back and forth slightly as I stared toward it. I tried to regain my composure with a deep sigh but to no avail.

Each time that the door moved, I could hear a slight creaking in the iron hinges that rotated with the door. My rational mind knew that there must be a window open within the room, but the heat that I could feel building in the house dictated that there could not be a window open and no breeze to move the door. I leaned toward the door and looked about the room, but could see no window open. However, there was a darkened figure that seemed to be sitting in the far corner of the room as if looking at something within its hand. I dared not move or make a sound as I was not sure what this being was or that it could be the demon that I had fought once already. It simply sat facing the opposite direction but filling the air around it with a darkened void that seemed too dark to peer through.

It seemed as if all light was being devoured around it and I could do nothing at this moment other than stare. I feared everything in the world at this moment and seemed to not be able to control my emotions. My mind tried to reason through the situation in a usual fashion by the thought that I might be asleep and dreaming, hallucinating everything, or the stress of this life was finally getting the better of my mind. None of these scenarios could satisfy me as nothing seemed to line up perfectly since the rest of the room was undisturbed and seemed normal. The walls were beautifully decorated with floral wallpaper that was covered here and there by paintings and other such decorations.

The bed in the far corner of the room looked just as it did when I bought the home with the most basic of dressings on it but was a gently carved oak wood that seemed to be

complemented by the flooring in the room which was a rougher hewn oak. There was also a wooden dresser that was set to the left side of the room directly across from a large window to the front of the home. A window beside the dresser faced out to the back lot of the home but was overshadowed by the thing in the corner.

I fought myself to move away from the door but feared taking my eyes off of this creature. Nothing could stop this imposing force from rising and grasping me and then dragging me to my death. I would not be able to stop any advances of harm or any end that would come my way if I were to make my presence known. Though I was not sure of what Mary would be doing in this moment or if she would be approaching the stairs and wondering why I had vanished. I was sure that she wondered why I had not brought the remaining luggage up from the entry of the home.

"Dear God!" I thought, *"What about Mary?"* as the horror crept into my mind. I

considered that she would be suspicious of what would be occupying my time. I quietly but quickly moved from the doorway and back down the stairs to the bottom landing. All the while hearing the faint sounds of toppling furniture and crashing paintings in the upper guest room. Just as I reached the bottom landing and moved toward the other luggage, Mary approached from the sitting room.

"I am trying to settle into this home, my love, but everything is so different and wonderful here," Mary said.

I replied, "I am glad that you feel welcomed here. I had worried that you would not like it here".

Mary seemed taken aback by my words as if she assumed that this was my normal home, but I was not willing to become embroiled in a conversation about that subject at this moment.

"I am working as quickly with the luggage as I can, dear. Would you prepare some whiskey for us? The bottle is in the lower cabinet of the curio piece," I said. I could not waste more time returning to the upper floor and making sure that this being was gone. Unfortunately, secrecy had to be the first thought in my mind if I wished to protect Mary from this evil.

I grasped all the luggage I could carry and moved toward the upper landing again. I was not sure what I would do to defend myself from this evil, but the luggage might make a grand weapon if even to just slow the being. Though I knew that even this would not stop such a creature. I could not allow myself to think of this being returning to haunt me as a defeat on my part, but rather a test of my sanity and resolve. More importantly, I was not sure how I would be able to stop anything from escalating as it did in North Carolina. I turned the corner and looked upward toward the door to the guest room and could see that the door was now closed.

Surely this was something that the demon had done to antagonize my mind or to make me think that everything was not as I had witnessed. I moved toward the top landing once again and approached the door only to notice an empty hall in the dim light of the upper level. I set the luggage down and placed my hand on the doorknob. With a twist to the left and then to the right, I was able to open the door gently and quietly, but there was nothing behind said door. No darkened being was sitting in the corner as if willfully ignoring me. This time, however, I would not be made a fool and I would enlist as much help as I could from anyone who might know something about this being.

I could no longer fool myself into thinking this being was something solely imagined, but instead was a true being that could move and harm anything that it wished. It seemed that there was more of a motive of torment and unease in the way that this being operated. Nothing was assured and I could not allow this demon to affect my life if I were to have peace and happiness. Instead, I moved into the master bedroom just across the hallway from this room and placed our luggage on the floor. Mary would be able to open her luggage and unpack later in the day before retiring to the kitchen. I was determined to keep her in my sights, to not offer her as an unwitting sacrifice.

I set the luggage near the wardrobe to the right of the door to the bedroom, but I kept my focus on the room across the hallway. Surely nothing would happen now and I would simply be on my guard for no reason. It seemed too predictable, although I had not felt any reason to think that anyone would be watching or following me. That was different from what I had experienced before and I was sure that this was the calm before the storm. I was not certain the being understood the level of fatigue that I held in my heart for being its toy. When this beast could no longer make me fear anything it would change and evolve its methods as it had in the past. I would simply wait and watch for the time to be right tonight for this demon to make itself known once more.

I knew this thing wanted me alone, wanted to devour all of my constitutions to make me bend to its will. I was not sure how I knew these things, but I just did since the dream that I experienced on the train. This wasn't something implanted within my mind from the beast itself, but I was sure that it was somehow related. *Could it be that this was less of a family curse and more of a dark pet called upon when my aunt or mother needed to defend themselves?* I could not be certain, but it was all beginning to seem more than a coincidence. Either I would find a way to defeat this demon once and for all or I would live with this darkness while attempting to keep it at bay.

The latter was the most alarming thought that I have had in a long time as it would imply that I would be a servant to this being and be complicit with evil. Before my mind drifted any further into this thought, I could hear Mary moving toward the center of the lower level. She was moving with light footsteps, but the creaking of the floor echoed into the corner near where I stood.

"The whiskey is ready, Benjamin!" She yelled up the stairs.

"I will be down in a moment!" I responded.

I quickly felt the excitement of a relaxing glass of whiskey enter my thoughts and I could do nothing to resist moving down the stairs. Though it was only fair that we move outside to sit under the back porch and converse as we drank and enjoyed the day. Mary had already seated herself with the windows open to feel the breeze. From outside the walls of the home, all manner of smells wafted through the windows and filled the room. It was the smell of fresh baked bread and meats being charred in the open air. I grasped both glasses of whiskey from the small, wooden table between the two sitting chairs in the room and began moving toward the door again.

"Come with me, my love. We will go to the back porch to sit in the open air." I said. Mary didn't seem to even consider fighting this suggestion as she simply stood and followed me to the back porch.

"I agree that it is a most beautiful summer day!" Mary stated excitedly.

I opened both doors and could see the most amazing view of a small pond in the far corner of the yard with stone walkways running throughout the backyard. The most magnificent flowers wafted in the wind with colors of gold, red, white, and purple. Mary and I both simply stood in the doorway of the home in amazement at the sea of beautiful plants. I had no idea that our home would be perfect for us as it was truly a purchase that I could be happy to have made. This home had been cared for in the most precious of ways which would cause Mary's heart to swell with excitement. The porch was a fine shield from the blazing heat and light of the sun as I had already removed my jacket and placed it on the coat rack when I entered the home which brought much relief.

The wind blew over the fencing positioned around the backyard and seemed to cause the flowers to dance in place, like ballerinas performing for an audience. I was interested at this point to know more about the people who called this place home before Mary and myself. They seemed to have an exquisite taste to put together such a beautiful home or were from a time when New York City was simpler and less crowded than now.

"My love, how was it that you came to buy this home? I thought that you were living in an apartment in the city." Mary asked.

I could not help but gaze into her beautiful hazel eyes and reply, "I was living in an apartment, but just before I left for North Carolina, I was approached by a coworker who asked if I was interested in buying property. I replied that I was as he explained that his parents had moved to another location and wished to sell this home. I viewed the home briefly, but I felt compelled to purchase it because I liked the home's coziness. I knew that it would be more fitting for me than an apartment".

Mary nodded and said nothing for some time while she sipped her whiskey and stared outward toward the yard. I could feel that her mind was racing with questions; some that I wished for her to ask and some that I did not wish to hear. My mind also raced with questions but none that Mary would be able to answer as it was in these moments that I wished to converse with Percy as our conversations always had a clearing effect on the mind. Yet I knew that no answers could come from anyone but myself and what I could investigate about this being.

"I am also happy with this home because it is simple but elegant. I just worry that the city would be a difficult place to live. Do you feel that it is important for me to be able to get an education here in the city?" Mary queried.

"I truly care nothing about what you wish to do with your time, my love. I am simply happy that you are here by my side and just wish for you to better yourself in any way that you can while moving forward with your life. Is that agreeable?" I replied.

Mary seemed to be taken slightly off guard by my statement, but she tried adamantly to hide her emotions. She knew that this was more than a life of hard labor and always having to wake at dawn to traverse muddy fields and care for animals of all kinds. This was a life with which she would be able to do more learning and discovering of who she was and what she wished to do in her life. I was not capable or able to stand around as Mary moved about her day to judge her every action as I was more concerned with working and trying to figure out my other issues in life. Trust had to factor into our relationship in a much more active role than others would like.

The sun had begun to sink behind the buildings that set across from our backyard while the light had started to fade. We knew that it was time for us to unpack our things and prepare for the next day, but this was not at the forefront of our minds. Instead, we enjoyed the last sips of whiskey and continued to converse in our usual fashion. Mary had surprised me with her ability to hold her liquor but it was starting to show that she was having issues being coherent in a conversation. Yet she still sipped on the last drops until there was nothing left of her glass. She was determined, to say the least, but still beginning to show signs that she was not able to function well. I stood and offered my hand to her which, at first, she seemed to refuse, but realized that she needed the help. I hoisted her up from her chair and assisted her inside before shutting the back door. We moved to the upper level for much desired rest after a long day of travel.

3

The next day began as any other, with the sun rising as Mary and I lurched out of bed. We stumbled to gather our clothes and dress for the day ahead. It was not known what we would be doing or if we wished to leave our home. Nothing was assured on a day such as this and it seemed as if we had been given a blank slate which gave me comfort in a very profound way. I knew that Mary would be eager to leave home and search out the sites within the city, but it would have to simply wait for another day as we were to spend this time getting settled. I felt the excitement within the room as Mary slipped her last shoe onto her foot and seemingly jumped with joy. This was behavior that I had found uncharacteristic of anyone within the stuffy city, as others were too concerned with image and normality.

Mary was a breath of fresh air and perspective, which gave my heart hope for the future and everyone within it. Perhaps it was our oddities that moved the world forward rather than the common man, trudging along plodded streets only to find themselves in the same spaces as the day before. I did not know the answer to this postulation, but I was sure to find out when living with a woman such as

Mary. I knew that she would be able to bring out a change within those around her and the people who would never see a different world, otherwise. Mary was a little plucky with a hint of curiosity and I could not help but want her within my space at all times to learn and share with her. I watched as she moved with such speed, grace, and excitement toward the door of our bedroom then wrench the doorknob to one side and yank the door toward her.

She was like a wraith floating down the small corridor on the upper floor before seeming to hover down the stairs to the lower landing. It was all that I could do to follow her without falling to the floor in excitement, but I held myself together. I moved at a normal pace down the steps to the bottom and witnessed the oddest sight. Mary was amazed to see that the light had filtered into the front windows in such a way as to cast the shadow of a hulking form upon the ground. It was darker than any shadow around it, yet it seemed completely normal. I rushed forward and stood upon the shadow as it darted to one side of the door and then vanished into a closet doorway within the sitting room. The shock of this sight was alarming, to say the least, as I could not understand what had just happened. I was confused as to how I could feel a shadow as it moved from under my foot with an abrasive trembling as it moved.

Nothing could have prepared my eyes for this sight and my mind could not process anything that I had witnessed. Mary seemed to notice nothing but was stunned at my reaction within the moment while she stared at me with the most peculiar look on her face. She looked toward me as if wondering if I had lost my mind.

"I thought a bug had scurried within our home, my love. My apologies for my behavior as I did not mean to alarm you." I spoke.

Mary said nothing for a moment then moved into the sitting room. She looked about the room as if wondering which seat to take. I was not sure how I would continue to hide such events from her attention, but I was determined to do so stubbornly. As I saw Mary take her seat, I could not help but desire to sit with her and partake in a conversation that would never end. I longed to move within her range and embrace her as a new love then kiss her passionately until she could no longer resist me.

I knew that this was not something that needed to take place at a time like this, but I was more ready than ever to embrace her whole being. I had been dumbfounded at the idea that I would be so smitten with a woman in my life. I knew that such strong desires existed within this realm, but I had thought it the work of Shakespeare or poets long since deceased. Surely my heart would not be devoured by this blind devotion to this young woman for carnal needs only. Surely this was a divine calling that grasped my heart every day upon seeing Mary. These were the strings that pulled within my heart to make me realize that I would do anything to protect Mary from this beast. Especially so if I were to find that it had formed a new lair within this home.

Certainly, any sane person would not fault a man for protecting his new bride in such a noble and dignified way. After all, it was not as if I had gambled our fortune away nor had I been able to lay with another woman on any given night. I knew not what anyone would do in my situation, but I knew that I had to play a better hand against such a cunning foe which meant employing the help of a loyal friend. Luckily I had such a friend in mind when it came to things that I could not understand. Perhaps I would be able to slip away from Mary in the coming days to handle my business while also paying a visit to Edric. He was the sort of friend who did not wish to become embroiled in another's affairs but would supply a wealth of information on any subject that was desired.

Edric is not the sort to abandon those that would need him, however, while also not becoming embroiled in a cause that he didn't believe in. Edric was also a friendly sort that could hold confidentiality on anything that was spoken within his company. He had always guided me on any subject that I desired and always had a wealth of artifacts on hand to showcase his talents for gathering information about history. I had come to know such a man whilst researching within the university's library one fine evening. I would always race to the library after any day of working within the bank and begin avidly reading up on the subject that my mind had pondered most.

I was always careful with any volume on the shelf and would never remove or replace a book hastily to not damage the covering in any way. It was this behavior that first endeared Edric to me and with haste. He had approached me on a rather snowy evening when I could not sleep on a long night. He placed a bottle of whiskey upon the table beside me along with two glasses and said, "My fine fellow, what brings you here on such a dreadful night? Shall it be the written word and the knowledge that it contains to fill your mind with warmth and light?"

How he would speak caught me off guard but went a long way to ease my racing mind then he would finish with something quite intellectual. I knew then that this man would become a close friend, especially when sharing a fine whiskey on a dreary and cold night. Since that time, I had leaned upon the vast knowledge that Edric held within his mind. He was also a scholar on games of the old world as well as items of the occult and esoteric teachings. Surely anyone would be able to lose themselves in a conversation with this man and then be drawn back to reality by his hospitality. I decided then that it was imperative that I visited Edric on the subject of this demon and anything that it wished for Mary and me.

I was intent on allowing Mary settle into our home after such a long journey across the countryside, however. This was a place that I had hoped would be a symbol of comfort and joy for my beautiful wife and any children that we chose to have within its walls. I also know that Mary would become the next target for such a horrible creation and surely would not have the fortitude to endure such torture. After all, I, myself, have suffered deeply in my own heart after the horrors that came upon me in North Carolina. I needed to move quietly and swiftly throughout my day and then leave when Mary would least suspect it. There was no evidence to say that my nightmare on the train would be from this being, but my heart said otherwise. Nothing would make more sense than to suffer within my dreams to bring this being to our new domain.

I turned to witness Mary looking about the home with a child-like disposition as I had never seen within her before. She was truly a gentle and beautiful soul and a person who could not be contained within a singular description with a gentle mind who could not be bothered with darkened things. Mary was one of a kind and she truly appreciated all that we had achieved in our lives currently. I simply watched her move about the home and look at the furniture along with the wood paneling of the dining room. Light gently filtered into the room from the morning sun between the curtains that had been pulled slightly closed. Shadows had formed perfectly within the space to accent the best angles within the room. I could see that Mary had a desire for expensive tastes just as I had acquired after moving my life to New York City.

I had hoped that she would enjoy the decor that I had sourced from within the city and placed in our home. Now I stood within the entryway, watching the woman whom I could not separate myself from, moving through the home and enjoying the beauty of it. I too had begun to enjoy the space as well since I no longer was forced to live within a simple and less inviting apartment deeper into the city. I was happy indeed to have purchased the home to make money on real estate and then having a home when needing one on such short notice. The only issue that I could take with the home, was the cleaning that would need to be done to maintain its quality. I would make it a point on this day to find a maid who could become a nanny for any children that would be born. I did not wish to make such a deal with anyone until I could ensure that this demon had not traveled with Mary and myself to New York. There could be no scenario in which I would be comfortable with another person being tormented by this demon for no reason.

When I returned to reality, Mary was moving into the sitting room with a most pleasing look on her face. I could not stop myself from interjecting into the moment, "Is our new home to your liking, my love?"

Mary did not turn toward me at first and continued to look about the space before looking toward me with a pleasant smile and replying, "I am very pleased my love. This home is gorgeous and I feel as though I could enjoy my life here in the city,"

These remarks made my heart beat at a quickened pace within my chest as I had never felt before. It eased my mind to know that Mary would be this approving of a home that I had purchased by chance a year ago. I found these growing coincidences more than I could handle at times, but I was sure to remember that my mind was being acted upon by outside and negative forces as well. The coupling of these factors gave rise to questions of what was real in my world and perception. I did not believe with any rational thought that I was being subjected to a horror that had been contrived from false memories or a psyche that had shattered long ago. Instead, I was keenly aware that what I had experienced was not a fantasy or falsehood implanted in my mind, but a fact of the life that I was now living.

Mary could not understand and I did not wish to bring her into this reality for no reason other than some circumstance forcing my hand. Mary will not understand anything that I would tell her until she experiences the same. This demon has a keen awareness of how to make you second guess yourself until you give in to its desires and way of thinking. As I stood in the kitchen watching Mary move about the room and prepare delicious meats for breakfast. The aromas were accented by the earthy scent of potatoes soaked in butter. She moved with the grace of a dancer, to and fro with the timing of the symphony from the sounds of cooking. She was truly an artist with unparalleled skill in the kitchen and with any food items it seems. The aroma of the room swirled together only to collide with my olfactory sense which made my mouth water instantly.

I could almost taste the inevitable bouquet of flavors that would accompany such delicious meats. There were cuts of beef and small slivers of pork with seasonings that I could not understand. None of these cuts were whole as we had not purchased such, but it was enough to satisfy our hunger. It was with good fortune that Mary and

I would arrive early in the day to purchase such modest culinary items.

Mary lovingly scooped the juices emitted from the meat onto the potatoes to not allow the tubers to dry out while sitting in the pan. She also seasoned the meats generously but not so much that the seasoning would diminish the natural flavor of the meat. I could not describe the excitement that I could feel while waiting for the delicious food. I still found a way to enjoy this show, as well as the bitter taste of a glass of whiskey, whilst Mary worked away for our sustenance. I knew that this was a love of hers but she was modest toward her skills as a cook. I had learned a great many skills when I was younger but never held an affinity for cooking in the way Mary had.

Yet I knew that I had become wealthy enough so to not force Mary to work away on such skills unless she chose to do so each day. I wished to become much more wealthy as the owner of The Northeast Bank, but I simply was not sure if Mr. Sorghum would wish to sell the property. I knew, through my many dealings with the man, that he had wished to rid himself of the headache. He was a man who held many properties but did not have the same difficulty in claiming profits on those spaces. You see, this was the only business that Mr. Sorghum had difficulty maintaining as it was an older building.

I could understand the frustration that he held as our bank seemed small and was unable to maintain steady clients until I had taken over as head banker, but he never seemed content. Mr. Sorghum had not anticipated that I would be able to bring in such profits and entertained a concerted effort to repair the grounds. He eventually relinquished this notion as the foundation had not been sound and needed more care than most. Water had begun to erode some of the pipework under the building which then hastened the degradation.

These were the only issues plaguing the bank, but it was nothing that a short time of remodeling the bank inside and out would not be able to solve. Though I did understand that this would be a massive undertaking. The lot was sound and the building would be able to house anything that any developer would need, even apartments. I had no intention of turning the building into such, but it was a nice thought to acquire various properties. I wished to have a hand in developing this city further while using the profits that I could manage from the bank as the anchor that could launch an empire of real estate. Now my years of getting estimate after estimate under the nose of Mr. Sorghum would pay off as I had finally heard a quote that would please both my mind and my pocket without sacrificing the building itself.

My mind then turned to Mary moving through the kitchen and plating our food rapidly in such a way as a master chef would do. I could not help myself while salivating at the thought of tasting this medley. We then moved into the dining room and took our places at the table across from each other. She had placed my food in front of me and then in her place as I pulled her chair out for her to rest comfortably within it. She then swept her dress to one side and slowly lowered herself onto the seat. She was rugged, graceful, and beautiful all in the same way which culminated in a woman who could be trusted with any issue. It was a taboo subject within our polite society to talk about the contributions of women in our society, but that was beginning to change. It was the right of every man and woman to enjoy the lives that God had produced as a vessel for our spiritual education upon this earth.

Mary had become comfortable as I rounded the end of the table and took my seat. We then picked our utensils from their places and began eating. Each item that I placed in my mouth was a cacophony of flavors that all danced across my tongue to produce the sweetest flavors. Too long have I become accustomed to eating within a parlor while waiting for a shave or a haircut while missing the taste of a lovingly prepared meal. My mother had been the cook of my childhood home and I had become accustomed to such a way of living until I moved myself to New York City. Yet I still ate while sitting on the molding just below the window of my apartment before meeting such a fine woman as Mary. I longed to have the meals my mother could prepare.

Reminiscing would inevitably be accompanied by the memories

of watching my mother slowly waste away in her bed shortly after laying my father to rest. I had never known the true extent of what had happened to my father, but my mother had simply stated that I was too young to understand such things and that accidents had occurred. I did not take kindly to these answers as they seemed bureaucratic in every sense of the word. It seems as if my mother had taken a measure of skepticism with the words that she had spoken to me about the subject. Knowing what I had begun to understand when within North Carolina, I could not help but wonder if she or my aunt had something to do with my father's death. Surely this was an unfounded worry, but I could not stop my mind from pondering such things. The worry then flooded into my mind that this being had claimed the man who had sired and helped raise me and then had taken my mother to the same fate.

Mary could not have known anything that drifted through my thoughts as I simply produced the coldest and stony face that one could muster to keep the peace through my life. She was a woman keen in every sense of the word and knew many things that no one could have spoken to her. This was something that she had never described to me, but her family could all do the same. They had hailed from Colombia in South America, but being within these lands had begun removing these traditional abilities from them.

She had complained many times that her family was no longer able to share their native customs and language. Time was cruel to such memories and this new life had demanded nothing from these people in the way they had been accustomed. I had met many whilst living in the city who could say the same thing about their lives now as opposed to the life that they had once lived outside America. This new world had different expectations and demands that seemed to cause such people to become less reliant upon their old customs and traditions. It was a sickness of the heart that remained within these people as they had grown fond and homesick of their old ways.

I understood such sadness deeply as I felt the same when I lost my family, yet I can never go back to that life or those customs. I have nothing left of my old ways nor the knowledge of how to perform such rituals within my own life. My language had faded and begun to dissipate within my heart and it seemed that I could never rekindle such a flame. I could feel sadness for such a loss but a feeling of joy and comfort in the things that I had been willing to sacrifice for the new life that I had achieved. Mary broke these revelations within my mind by saying,

"My love, are you going to leave the home at any time today?" I stopped what I was doing and then shook my head at first, but distinctly felt a nod wishing to escape me. Her voice reached my ears again.

"I will be fine here without you, husband. I will settle in while you attend to your matters. There is no reason to stay here with me and I am sure you have business to which you must attend," Mary stated calmly.

These were the moments in which I knew that Mary could sense more than she would allow anyone to know, but I could not argue with her reasoning. I knew that today would yield many more treasures if I were left to my own devices within this great city. I also knew that I would have to balance my time to allow Mary the ability to see something within these new surroundings.

As I finished my meal and kissed Mary goodbye, I felt the need to take her to the parks that were scattered throughout the city which gave leisure to those residents near them. No such place existed in our area of the city, but it was not a long journey to the nearby fountains and parks. I felt it best to allow Mary to get some fresh and cool air on such a warm day. I closed the door behind me and hailed a coach to take me further into the city and to my place of employment. I knew that the bank would need a reason to continue without its head banker and I would provide them with such. I knew that it would be no issue at all to mention that I would be taking a trip to Mr. Sorghum's home to make an offer for the bank, but I would keep these matters private. I knew that he might enter the bank at any moment throughout the day and overhearing my offer prematurely could allow him to consider a ludicrous counteroffer.

I did not wish to deal with these objections to my want to

purchase the bank and I would not allow myself to be drained of cash in such an oppressive way. Surely a couple of extra days would be no issue with anyone who worked in the establishment. I was sure to not allow any such bluff to be witnessed upon my face until I could remove myself. Once I had arrived outside the bank, I made a point to enter the building and greet everyone that I could. Questions followed shortly as to my trip and how I had fared, but I did not allow this to slow my progress. I met with the Associate Manager of the bank to inform him that I would be back in the next few days unless something were to change. No questions were asked as to why and I would not allow myself to tell anything that was to be kept secret.

It was not long before entering the same coach again and traveling the route to Mr. Sorghum's home for our negotiation. I worried that he would not be available and I would not be able to complete my business, but the butler offered another suggestion as he led me into the deeper portions of the immaculate home. The decorations and furniture were of a high quality which had been matched to the smallest details. Everything had been themed in white and gold within and lit very well with finely crafted candle hangers. The art and sculptures held within seemed too fine for a private home and were sure to have entered a museum at one time or another in its existence.

Even the gardens in which Mr. Sorghum and his wife were seated held such opulence that I could hardly believe that I had not stepped into an ancient castle or king's palace. I could not stop the feeling that I did not belong inside this home while appearing so meager compared to my surroundings. I felt lifted, however, by seeing such a living space and knowing that I could obtain such a lifestyle for Mary and myself. These thoughts were broken by laughter and flirtatious speech as I turned my head to the left and was met with Mr. Sorghum and his wife standing to greet their new guest. I was embraced heartily by both then seated across from them.

"What brings you to our fine home this morning, Mr. Price?" asked Mr. Sorghum.

I hesitated to allow the words to escape my mouth for fear of rejection at first. Then I simply forced myself to breathe deeply and then push out the words that I could never imagine myself saying.

"Mr. and Mrs. Sorghum, I wish to purchase the bank from you and eliminate your worries about caring for such a place," I said confidently and with a smile.

I had imagined that Mr. Sorghum would have objected in some small way to this idea when I had previously imagined the interaction, however, he did not.

"I would be glad to accept any offer that you present to me, Mr. Price! I have had my eyes on you for some time and I realize that you are a man who could not be contained. You have a love for banking and business comes easily to you. I would be proud to know that I have sold this property to welcome a new wealthy resident into this city." Mr. Sorghum stated.

My mind could not fathom this response and I was sure that he had spoken in jest, but his face said otherwise. I reeled for something to say to such a statement, but I could find no words to satisfy my mind and heart on this matter.

"Simply tell me your amount and my bookkeepers shall draw the documents to be signed when you have the time to come by the bank." He added.

I did not know what to say yet again as this was all happening so easily, but my mind forced me to speak to not appear as a bumbling imbecile in front of such a connected man.

"I would offer you sixty thousand dollars for the building and pay for any repairs on my own as I have a contractor whose quote is very adequate to repair the building in its entirety," I replied.

Mr. Sorghum laughed heartily, "Sixty thousand? That is not the offer that I thought you would make but it is too much for that space in my mind. I would only accept fifty thousand for such an establishment. After all, you know my difficulty when it comes to maintaining the building as well as the staff. I will also let you know that I have not received the payment of profit from the building for this month so you would be able to collect that. Now come here and shake my hand!"

Mr. Sorghum continued to laugh, a deep belly laugh, as he accepted my handshake and drew me in for an embrace, laughing all the while. I still seemed like a buffoon in his midst for I continued to struggle for the words to say.

This was most gracious on his behalf and I was determined now to make good upon my words. I had in my possession one hundred, thousand dollars to purchase and repair the building. Now I would be able to continue with payroll to start the purchase on an even footing. I could not fathom that Mr. Sorghum would wish to sell me this property for such a meager sum and I was sure that there would be an angle to this sale, but I could find none in my mind, at present. I simply thanked the man and his lovely wife then partook in a gathering with them and drank tea and enjoyed eloquent snacks all in the name of business.

This was to say that I had been eagerly entertained by the words that he spoke in regard to the bank and all that he had experienced while owning the business. He talked as though I had relieved him of a burden he had no idea what to do to resolve. I was sure he had contemplated collecting money on the building through unfortunate means. Though I had no evidence of this being the case. I was sure that he meant claiming the building as condemned and allowing it to slip into a sad state.

None of this mattered now, however, as I would now need to visit my contractor in a few days and inform him that his crew and he would have work for quite a while. Now I could hire a new head banker and then move into a much easier position as owner of the property. Mary would be ecstatic at this option and I would be proud to tell her of this accomplishment. The only time wasted would be that of waiting for the contracts to be drawn and the agreements to be signed.

After the conversation and subsequent gathering with Mr. Sorghum and his wife, I moved back to the street and walked the short distance down toward the city center then across another street and down an alleyway. There I would meet with Edric at his home and enjoy the true information that I needed at that point in my life. I knocked upon the door and awaited its opening eagerly, yet I held my composure on this matter as I did not wish to seem desperate.

Edric opened the door shortly and greeted me while bidding me to come inside the home. I did as he requested and waited for him in the foyer until he closed his present dealings. I was then greeted once more as we sat within the library of his home and his servant prepared tea in the late morning hour.

"What has brought you to my home on such short notice, Benjamin?" He asked.

By the time he had finished his sentence, I had begun to take a sip of my tea. Hurrying to swallow, I promptly replied, "I am here to discuss a most unusual matter with you, friend. I have learned much about my mother and aunt whilst visiting the manor in North Carolina and it pains me so. Would you know about anything within the realm of the supernatural or ultra-normal?" I said.

Edric thought for a moment as he took repeated sips from his tea and began speaking, but paused for a moment more.

"What is it exactly that you are asking of me, Benjamin?"

I began speaking immediately on the matter that consumes me at present while explaining what I had discovered in North Carolina that pertained to my mother and aunt. As usual, Edric said nothing at first and simply pondered the information that I had relayed to him. I could see that his endless pondering would not get the better of him, however.

"I have heard of something about your situation, but I am not privy to the rituals that you have described. However, I can tell you that this being does not have a name as others would, but it is defined all the same. I will look for the tome that you need, but you will have to give me a day or two at the most." He finished.

I accepted his offer and conversed with him about his thoughts on the matter while he offered some advice. He stated that it would be best to acquire salt and several white candles with parchment paper along with sage. Then I would be given the understanding of what to do with these items once he can visit me and bring the tome which I need. I thanked him for his help and stood from my chair while bidding him a good day. I then strolled across the floor calmly and out the front door. Edric had seen me out in the most tranquil manner as well. I could tell, however, that he was perplexed by the idea that his close friend would be plagued by such a haunting.

I then straightened my stove-pipe hat and gathered my cane that had been left in his entryway in my hand. It didn't take much for me to move back onto the sidewalk and begin heading for my own home. Along the way, I stopped and purchased delicious baked goods for Mary and I to enjoy with the good news. She would be overjoyed to have such a delightful conversation along with the prospect of elevating our family's wealth.

I was sure that Mary would have made our home more comfortable and would have begun preparing lunch by this time. I was privileged to have such a wonderful woman to work at home as I attended to my personal business and I was determined to meet her kindness of my own. I stopped by the grocers and purchased chocolates along with flowers for my lovely wife then strolled back to our home. It was nothing for me to feel empowered as I had been showered with good fortune upon my return to this great city. This was the start of the rest of my life and it was a very grand start, to say the least.

I opened the door gently and moved into our home gracefully and quietly. I had sneaked through the dining room and into the kitchen while making sure to check my surroundings for Mary to surprise her. Eventually, I found her standing on the back porch of our home and admiring the flowers that grew in our tidy garden. I moved silently behind her and put my arms around her whilst showing her the chocolates and flowers along with the baked goods. She shrieked with shrill excitement and turned to embrace me firmly while a warm smile moved slowly across my face. Mary was elated in the best way by the news that I had purchased the bank and would be moving into real estate as a dedication in life.

I would no longer be held by another man's successes and I would be able to have a slice of this great city for myself. Mary pulled me into our home and then into the kitchen to share in the chocolates and bakery treats. The baked goods were warm, soft and delicious, to say the least. We then sat down to a hearty lunch which left Mary and I pouring two glasses of whiskey and we finished our perfect day on the porch while watching the sun sink behind the buildings. Our paradise had finally been realized in much the way that I had imagined and I could not be more fulfilled at this time.

4

The night approached quickly as Mary and I shared multiple kisses and glasses of wine. It was then a chore to undertake the task of climbing the endless stairs back to our room for rest, but along the way, we had begun losing our clothing with haste. That is to say that we had left our clothing strewn across the whole of the stairway that led to the upper floor and entered our room completely bare. The night air felt cool as we began sharing the bed with our windows open wide to allow for our home to cool completely. I moved closer to Mary and began kissing and nibbling on her neck as I embraced her firmly within my arms. It was all that she could do to resist my charms and infectious touch while maintaining her composure. She was not a woman who wished to seem like a common street lady nor a tavern whore. No, she was a lady with wants and desires who needed just as she gave.

I continued to move my hands down her body and to her hips as her heart began pounding even more. I could feel each beat with my lips as I continued to kiss and nibble gently against her beautiful and supple skin. I could not wait any longer to have this amazing woman as I lay her gently upon the bed and aligned myself with her. One deep and slow thrust sent her into a world of immense passion and longing for the night to never end. I could feel her breath steaming against the skin on my ear as she moaned and breathed heavily. She was writhing underneath me more and more as I continued to hold her and caress her. I moved my arm under her right leg and lifted it slightly as I pushed completely into her and began thrusting firmly and rhythmically. Her flesh was for the taking and I was a man who desired to give her what she needed. I slid down and began tasting her until she lost her mind once more.

We both continued working against each other in this way until she could take no more and I completed our circuit of love by pushing deep and embracing her passionately within my arms until the only sounds were those of our breathing. We continued to embrace each other tightly for some time then lay with our arms folded across each other. Staying on our sides until we both had fallen asleep but nothing could have ended that day as perfectly and with such love and desire for each other and our flesh.

The world continued to turn until the night had fallen firmly upon our home. I only know of this as I had begun seeing us sleeping in this way with eyes that were not made of flesh and blood. I felt as though I were dreaming but my senses were that of someone who had been pulled from bed in a delirious state and without cause. I had not chosen to dream of this or actually be present for such horrors that would come next. I could hear a faint scratching upon the wood of our home underneath me, but I could not place from where it emanated. It sounded as if someone were scratching the very boards under my bed, but while also being in the same room.

This was the most alarming sensation that I could not stop and I could not understand with conventional means. My mind had been dulled and I could not process anything as quickly as I had before. It was as though I were in a dream but my body could still feel, in much the same way as if I were awake. I could hear the ghastly scratching accompanied by a faint moaning as though someone was being tormented. This caused my heart to skip several beats until I believed that I was dying. I realized that I had to be in a dream as I was alert and able to see my naked body laying beside Mary on the bed in front of me. Confusion did not seep into my thoughts as all seemed to be normal to my current state of mind. Nothing could be more clear than what I was witnessing before me right now.

I immediately rose from where I was and began moving toward the doors as I noticed that the room seemed to begin to grow larger and further away. No matter what I tried nor how hard I would run against this, I could not reach the door with any length of my arm. Instead, I was left to stand in horror as all of the boards around the door began to writhe and buckle on their own. They began flexing inward toward me as the door violently shook of its own accord. The sounds of cracking and buckling continued as I noticed that Mary and I had begun moving within our place upon the bed. I knew then that this was all happening and I was trapped within my mind and absent from my own body. *What had caused this to happen and was this affecting only me or had Mary been drawn into this as well? Surely this was all just a coincidence of an imaginative mind and I was not a part of this in reality.*

It was then that I realized that the door frame had begun slowly snapping free of the boards within the wall and the door had fallen into the room before it smashed down upon the footboard of our bed. The only thing witnessed on the other side of that awful opening was a darkness that had been blacker than the night itself. I could not see into it nor could I look beyond it and I seemed to be compelled to keep my eyes upon this form. The shape itself seemed to be amorphous and stretched across the whole of the doorway. Then tendrils stretched outward and had begun wrapping themselves around Mary as they seemed to grasp her body and yanked her off the bed slightly. I yelled out, "STOP IMMEDIATELY!" as the form continued to hold Mary in the air. I then moved toward it and began praying as I held my hands toward the tendrils and wished that they would leave Mary in peace, but to no avail. I was simply swatted against the wall and unable to recover whilst horrified to witness what came next.

I could do nothing but see Mary being slowly drawn into the darkness itself while I continued to scream and jerk against whatever force was holding me against the wall of the room. It was then that I had been tossed against the floor and moved toward my own body. I slapped my face and pushed against my flesh to awaken, but it was no use. I climbed upon my body and began savaging my face repeatedly until my flesh began to distort and change. My eyes opened to reveal that there were no eyes within these horrid sockets and only darkness remained. Then my lips began whispering something that I could not understand until I started to move closer. In that instant, an unsettling voice rang out in a woman's voice that was distorted and deepened.

"She is ours! You will be next, but we will keep your whore company until that time!"

The only thing left to hear was a cackling that continued for several minutes as the face continued to distort until it was that of my aunt's.

I held my hand out to the sky and yelled out, "God, hear me! Send this demon to whence it came and remove its foul presence from her body!"

It was then that I awoke suddenly and gasped for air while looking about the room only to notice that everything had been restored from this horrid dream. Mary had been placed back in the same spot where she had slept before and I was thankful. Surely I had found some sort of power within my dreams over this being and its reach.

I breathed a sigh of relief and then turned to look out of the window only to remember that my clothes and gun had been left outside of the door. My single-action had been placed halfway up the stairs and upon the bare wood itself. I worried that this being would seek to bring such an attack against me but would kill me with my own gun. This I would not allow as I moved from my place in bed and toward the door. I could feel flesh slapping against wood as I slowly worked my way toward the door and opened it. Caution stated that I should pause and wait to hear anything out of the ordinary. Nothing seemed to move or creak within our home as I slowly continued to the top of the stairs only to look down and see blackness before me. Only a dim sliver of moonlight shined through the window behind me and onto the wood of the stairs. I rushed to my gun and removed it from the steps only to lift it and grasp the handle firmly within my hand.

I could feel myself shaking slightly as the fatigue from my dreams had accompanied me back into my body upon waking. My finger rested off the trigger but was prepared to shift to the trigger and loose a bullet. I turned and began working my way back toward the top of the steps until I heard a creaking noise as though someone was walking on the floor of the lower landing. I turned and peaked around the corner with my pistol held outward and firm within my hand. My finger now rested on the trigger as I could feel the cold metal against my skin and I waited for anyone to peek around a corner. I knew that this would be the last time that they would peek around anything in their short lives as I would not have hesitated from taking theirs. My heightened state did not afford me anything but focus on this, however, as Mary placed her hand upon my shoulder and I jumped forward.

I landed on the lower floor and turned as I did while continuing to point my gun at Mary and froze. The silhouette of her moving within the darkened corner of the stairs caused my mind to scream out, "*Pull the trigger you damned fool!*"

I must admit that everything in me wished for this to happen, but I held firm that I would not until Mary emerged from the darkness. She seemed concerned and stood as I exhaled and lowered my pistol toward the ground. I backed against the thin wall beside me, trying to catch my breath.

"I am sorry dear, I thought that you were an intruder," I said while quivering from nervousness.

She moved toward me and took the gun from my hand then placed her lips against mine. I took her hand as she led me silently to the bedroom and we fell to sleep once more. I had not known what would have happened had I pulled that trigger and killed Mary, but I was thankful that I did not. My mind raced as I drifted into a lull and then back into a deep sleep, but I could not help but ponder what would happen now that I was falling into a restful state. *Would I be as helpless or would I be able to awake upon someone or something stirring within our home or our room?* I had no choice but to await the morning to find out what would happen next. Surely it would not be easy for anything else to happen now as I was sure that my prayer while being removed from my flesh worked against the power of this demon.

The morning light flashed into our room causing my face to crinkle due to the rays blinding me. I then reached over to caress Mary, but I could only feel crinkled sheets. I opened my eyes to see that she had left the room. This confused me because Mary would have surely awakened me while knowing that I would wish to be with her if she left the home. I suspected that she may have left the home without me and I rushed to wash off as best I could from the water bowl and then slipped into my suit.

My last steps seemed to come all too easily as I slid my gun into its holster under my vest and then placed a hat on my head. I then moved forward and out of our room only to find Mary standing in the hallway naked and facing the guest room of our home. She did not seem to notice that I was behind her nor that I had opened the door and walked across the wooden floor toward her. She seemed locked in a trance and I did not know how to rouse her. I slowly and gently moved my hand toward her then placed it upon her shoulder cautiously until she turned her head to see me out of the corner of her eyes. I straightened my collar and bowtie then looked up to see Mary's face differently as her eyes were now blackened holes in her face. Her mouth twisted then she stuck out a festering and darkened tongue toward me. I jumped back and leveled a shot from my pistol into her, but she did not move in the slightest.

Instead, she smiled and rushed toward me shrieking with the most heart-stopping sounds that I had ever heard. Upon seeing this I shot her again and again until she had reached me and begun snaking her tongue toward my eye. I was now staring into the empty holes that had been eyes within her skull while feeling her tongue move up my cheek and toward my eyes forcefully. I did not wait for any period before raising my single action to her chin and pulling the trigger for the last time. Mary's skull partially exploded and her forehead bulged outward as her tongue fell from my sight. I then dropped her onto the floor and stomped upon her head until it had crushed inward only to reveal a bundle of snaked what wriggled out of her and down the stairs.

I then felt the pressures that accompanied killing someone that I loved deeply. I collapsed to the ground once the realization set in that I had just killed Mary in such a grizzly way. Before I could bend down and cradle her body in my arms. I then awoke with a gasp and begin looking about the room. It was true that the sun shined around the room, but Mary had not moved from the place in which she slept. She still slept in much the same way that she had the night before. I could feel, however, that my mind had received more torment than rest throughout the night and I could not awake properly.

I quickly moved to my side of the room and backed myself into a corner while keeping my eyes upon Mary then slipped my clothes on once I knew that it was safe. My last action was to grip my pistol and place it within its holster on my vest. Mary had not begun to rouse at any moment while I performed any of these actions and I could not help but wonder why she had not moved in the least upon feeling me shift within the bed. She did not even shift in the slightest for several moments until I moved to her side and kissed her on her cheek. She then slowly opened her eyes and smiled while rolling within the bed then breathed in and out. She complained that her head hurt along with her right side only to roll again and see a bruise that had not been there in the night.

I held my tongue the best that I could and did not divulge what I had dreamt in the night, but she suspected much that had happened. She stated that she felt herself being lifted from the bed and taken somewhere dark and cold. Then she woke up for a moment and realized that I was gone only to move down the stairs until I shoved a gun in her face. I apologized for this and then helped her out of the bed and place clothes on herself. She then had trouble moving down the stairs as she complained about the pain in her side. Mary continued to mention that it seemed as though something was moving within her skin underneath the bruise but was still determined to go about her day. I could understand this and I did not try to convince her differently, but simply reminded her that I would have to leave to bring groceries home for us.

She smiled and thanked me for such as I moved toward the door. I then grasped my cane and opened the door only to hear the pouring rain outside.

"Goodbye my love, I shall return with the groceries. Try to rest yourself."

Releasing the handle after closing the door, I pulled my hat tighter upon my head. I trudged through the storm until I had come to the grocers. Perhaps it was me or a sense that I did not know I possessed, but I felt as though something had been different about Mary. I wished that I could have said that she was no different from any other time, but she was and I could sense it.

I could feel the darkness growing within Mary that no one would be able to understand other than those touched by the same darkness. I felt it stalking through our home last night, but I could not consciously understand it nor could I halt it in the least. Instead, I simply watched as Mary fell victim to it which had been confirmed by what Mary had stated. She was a sweet and gentle woman, but the way that she had acted when she first awoke was out of character for her. She spoke slightly differently and seemed to have a force to her words.

Her voice sounded grating and caustic in my ears, but I could not call it out as I knew that she would just wave it off. Mary was not the type to become hysterical about anything, but I was sure that even she could see that she had been attacked in the night. Surely I would know more upon my return home whether I would have to call a priest or not. I rounded the corner and moved to the front door of the grocer's as I straightened my hat and then opened the door. I stepped inside before I was greeted by the man behind the counter. I simply slid the list of what I had needed for that morning across the counter then I stepped back slightly.

"I have all of these items, sir. Allow me some time and I will collect them for you. I thank you," the grocer stated confidently.

It was then that the grocer moved to the back of the store and began moving a sack from the floor to the front counter of the store then plopped it upon the wood surface before moving to grasp other items. This all culminated in him taking his place on a ladder that had been attached to a slat of wood at the top of shelves upon the wall. He slid the ladder down just slightly with his foot then ascended it to grasp four more items before descending again and placing everything on the counter. Luckily most of the items were small enough to carry within one bag then place the sack of coffee under my other arm. I quickly paid the man what he had asked and then left the store only to find that the rain had hastened. I moved quickly toward our door only to slide my hand inside my pocket and remove a key.

I slid the key into the hole and turned the lock only to feel as if someone had been watching me. Yet, when I would turn to see who it would be, I saw nothing and nothing out of the ordinary. This made my stomach turn and the blood run cold in my veins as I opened the door and moved inside while slamming and locking it behind me. Mary approached me and asked if everything was in order and I had no answer for her. I did not wish to compound any issues by speaking them aloud only to be proven a victim of paranoia. I simply pushed the incident from my mind and placed the items from the grocer on the counter then moved back into the sitting room to light my pipe. I could feel a slight tremor within my right wrist as I lifted the match into the bowl of the pipe.

I could not forget this demon in any capacity, it was always waiting for me beneath the surface of my thoughts and I was not sure that I could contain it any longer. Sweat began to bead down my face rapidly until I heard the popping of the tobacco within the bowl and inhaled. In a rush of peace and misery, my thoughts became my own for the first time in several moments.

I could no longer be sure but my mind was being weighed upon heavily the further that I would travel through these thoughts. This terror flooded my life when I least needed such things, it gnawed at the back of my mind continuously until I felt as though my thoughts would burst forth from my mouth. Mary approached from my right as I puffed away on my pipe, but I did not notice her. I simply sat in this chair and gazed upon the rain that washed from the roof of our home and into the streets.

The occasional person moved swiftly past the window trying to dodge the bulk of the rainfall that pounded onto the streets. My mind did not receive the sounds of the pouring rain upon our roof and instead seemed to be blocking all sound. Only the hum of my thoughts could be heard over the world that I observed. That is until Mary placed her hand gently upon my right arm and then said, "Benjamin? Are you all right?"

I said nothing at that moment and simply stared out the window until I could feel the words welling up from my stomach and coming from my lips.

"I am well, my love, just thinking about something. Are you well?"

Mary gave me a look of disbelief, but it was short-lived until she replied with a heartfelt answer, "I am as well as I can be. Anything that I can do for you, my love?" I simply shook my head as Mary invited me into the dining room to enjoy a beef stock soup that she had just finished on the stove.

When I stood and approached the table, I was met with a lovely setting for Mary and myself to have an intimate lunch in a dimly lit dining room, but it all seemed a little too perfect for my mind. I had not become suspicious of Mary or her cooking, but the seeming peace that was within our home. I knew that it was only a matter of time before this peace was shattered and I was left worrying yet again for our safety. I found it horrid and somewhat beautiful how life could go from such success and happiness to fear and horror lurking around every corner, but it was as such. I took my seat at the table after allowing Mary to reach hers then scooting her under the table as well. The soup seemed murky and darker than usual, but I assumed that she used bone marrow as well as meat drippings to make the soup.

One sip after another went down my throat, but it all seemed off in texture and taste. Mary smiled and I could see blood beginning to trickle from her lips. I could do nothing at first except sit and watch in horror as she began asking me what was wrong with me. I looked down at my soup only to see a blackened hand reaching from within the liquid toward me. I felt warm water leaving my ears and nose as well as the corners of my mouth until I noticed that blood had begun to pour out upon my lap. I could stop nothing nor do anything as I fell out of my seat. I could feel my heart beginning to beat faster and faster until I could feel nothing else. I knew that I was being grasped from the inside of my person and attempts were being made to remove me from this reality. I reached out as I screamed only to feel the hands of my twisted wife pulling at it.

It was then that I could feel two large claws grasping my chest and pulling me into the floor and then down into the crawl space under the structure. I could do nothing to stop it save fighting my way to the top. Instead, I felt my body give in to these demands and I closed my arms across my chest to allow myself to be pulled deeper into the ground. Darkness surrounded me until I felt to be no more than a corpse laying within a broken coffin. The soil around me was damp and cold to the touch. My mind was flooded with images of my past and future, yet each one seemed confused and out of place, but they all seemed to be with someone else besides me living them.

I could not understand this being that had taken my place nor what it symbolized, but I had no control over leaving this place or stopping this nightmare. Yet I could still feel that something was coming for me around every corner of each vision. Eventually, it settled on Mary as darkened hands reached from behind her with each new memory that I witnessed. I called out for her to listen, but no one could hear a word that I was yelling until I could see a blackened heart beating within her chest. Her brilliant light had been taken and diminished until she was a shell of herself as I seemed to become younger and more full of life. Then I awoke with a yell and grasped at Mary's scarf around her neck pulling her down to me. Mary screamed in pain which brought me back into focus as I let go of her hair in an instant.

"What is the matter, my love?" She yelled out.

"I do not know, but I am sure that it is not good, my love." I replied, "I have taken a trip to where I do not belong and I am sure that I am not wishing to return there."

Mary said nothing at first but simply stared into my eyes until she could see that I was not disturbed then helped me to my feet. My mind raced with meanings and understanding of what had just happened. I was sure that the rest of our day would be just as chaotic, but I was resolute to allow no further control of my mind or my being. I simply placed myself back into my seat and began sipping my soup once more. This time, however, Mary would stare at me cautiously as I continued to pretend that nothing had occurred. I could feel my pulse and my heart slowing until I had returned to my normal self again, but I was still focused on trying to finish my meal.

I could feel a sense of unease creeping over Mary as she sat in silence and continued to eat her soup while keeping one eye trained on me. I could feel her gaze falling upon me without relenting until I had sipped the last of my soup and she was enabled to collect our dishes and return with the next portion of the meal.

She placed my meal in front of me and then in front of herself as I stood to help her be seated. She had lovingly prepared a potato and vegetable medley with a side of beef. The meat was a slab that seemed thick and juicy beyond any meal of which I had been able to partake. I began with the potatoes and then finished with the large piece of beef that had begun to leak delicious juices all over my plate. I had been fortunate to have a wife who had been able to prepare such a meal and bring about loving nourishment. It would be all that I would need to combat this force of evil.

Mary seemed worried about my well-being but I could tell that she wished to remain calm for this time as we both enjoyed lunch together. My mind still raced with questions, but I was sure that I would find the answers in time. The only fear that I held in my heart was that of her finding out about what was happening within our home. As well as our life which would be hidden save for these occurrences of me being infiltrated by evil itself. Surely this would be alarming to her on a deeper level and I did not wish to defend myself in some late evening conversation about my health and visiting a doctor to diagnose my ailment. I could not and would not allow a doctor to become involved unless I had no other choice in the matter.

Perhaps it was not going to move in that direction, but I could not be sure as I had fallen upon the ground and had no other option but to flail about for help. I had not been stricken with insanity, but these times were not helpful. Superstition lurked around every corner to condemn those who were odd or abrasive to the larger culture. Though I could not say that insanity, in one form or another, did not exist within my family or life.

5

Mary and I finished our filling and delicious lunch only to move onto the back porch and enjoy our drinks over a pipe. She did not usually partake in tobacco, but I could tell that she wished to enjoy the things that I would on a day such as this. We both discussed many things from our past as well as how fortunate we had been to have a home. The wind had begun to howl through the alleys in the buildings and homes around us, but it seemed to build and then die again before becoming any serious gust. Mary and I, however, were in complete comfort as we discussed our day and the associated perspectives. I know now that Mary had a delightful day without the torment of any hellish ghouls stalking her around every corner. I wished that I could share these experiences with Mary, but it would not be fortuitous to our relationship or her peace of mind.

Instead, we talked as though nothing odd had even happened all day yet we both knew of the events at lunch. No amount of pipe smoking nor whiskey would be able to erase the memories that I now carried within my mind that tormented me daily. Should it be that this haunting would culminate in my death, I would welcome it over the memory of such torments. Mary would wish for nothing less than peace for me in any case, but I doubted so with an untimely demise.

Surely she would wish for her husband to be safe even if it meant that he would live with darkness creeping through his mind.

I turned to Mary and said, "I would never be able to hide anything from you, my dear. There are things, however, that you would never wish to know. Our lives are going to change forever and I am no longer sure how to stop this. I am not well and so my life shall follow. I just hope to keep your life removed from any decisions that I should make in the coming days."

I could see Mary's face change dramatically to that of a darkened lust and I could not help but feel a stabbing fear within my heart. There also emanated an animalistic growl from her throat that seemed to indicate a lust for something if not blood or violence. Her eyes seemed to glow slightly with a dim yellow and widened with intense emotion. I could not help but withdraw my hand from near her and gaze into her face for a moment. As the rain began to fall much heavier and lightning crashed in the distance. I could not help but commit this sight to memory and allow my skin to recoil with bumps across its surface which gave me pause in speech and move-ment. I was not sure what to expect in the coming moments, but a chilling terror flooded up my spine and into the back of my mind.

Instantly I had become phobic of sound or movement and I could not help but wonder if Mary had fallen prey to this beast after all. Surely she has not fallen into the clutches of such a being without me knowing the signs, but I felt that my hunch had been correct when she was attacked within my dreams. Mary now showed the signs that she had been infected by this being in some small way and that my dream had a basis in reality. I worried for her as sorrow and empathy flooded my heart and a warm feeling washed over me. The love of my life had now been brought into this war and I felt that there was nothing I could do for her.

My initial reaction was to register her with the asylum, but I took the more resigned approach which was to wait this out and see what other signs began to show. I would then begin an experiment into finding out what ailed Mary and I would start with the most outlandish idea to the most. This would be the most interesting and sorrow-filled night of our marriage or it would be that fear would be expelled from my mind completely. I feared that Mary would suffer in any regard yet I could not understand how this would come about if this were a mundane lapse in rationale. My heart, however, spoke of ill tidings and portends of dark things to come. I could feel that Mary was not within her mind at this instant, but such things must be proven to me.

I knew all too well the issues of sending my wife to an institution at this time. These dwellings were often harsh to their tenants and unfair to the women and men who felt such misery. Houses of the Insane were no place for someone like Mary and I refused to turn her over to such inadequate care. This would have to be in a place that I could easily visit for her to receive the care needed without abuse. This was the fear that now surfaced within the oceans of thought washing about with my skull at any time. Waves of reluctance washed atop the shore of my resolve. After all, I could not care for such outbursts as I had witnessed from other individuals within the walls of such facilities.

Not only was it the belief that I must adhere to when dealing with the safety of my wife, but I was not resigned to simply forgetting who Mary had been. I wished to assist her health in any way that I could. Though, I did not have the heart to simply take her to such an establishment and leave her to fate itself. These times were hard for those who needed such care and abuse or neglect often awaited these patients when entering such a place. In my eyes, Mary was delicate and did not need anyone to attempt to harm her. Any woman could defend herself from many things, but to be allowed to attack someone who is not in their right mind with medications and inhuman treatments just to gain control over them and their state of being. This could not stand for anyone who claims to love their wife without end but resigned her to a fate worse than death and forget she exists.

I knew that the first course was to send for a doctor in the city in the morning and allow an examination of Mary for anything out of place. Perhaps a visit to a church after such time before moving on to the more extreme measures. Abandonment was not an option for me and my heart could not allow such abuse of Mary and her person. The only thought in my mind now was to be sure that I could come to an understanding should the worst present itself. The fear still lingered that she might be taken over by an unholy host as well, but I did not wish to fall into such hysteria in short order. I could be of no use to my lovely wife if I could not keep my wits about me in hard and uncertain times.

Mary had begun calming herself until she returned to a lucid and cooperative state. I pulled against her hand as I pulled her into our home to rest. She rested in the sitting room as I prepared a cup of tea for her, but a coffee for myself. I hoped that a soothing drink would allow Mary to calm her mind and slip into comfort. The coffee had a robust and harsh flavor but energized my body as no other.

I preferred fine-aged whiskey to drink in the evenings rather than a rough dessert drink such as coffee. I deemed it so that I would hold fast to the elder traditions without giving way to novel ideas toward beverages. I could see that Mary was thoroughly enjoying her tea, but probably more than she should at this time of day. The sun seemed to begin setting while being hidden only by clouds and rain. The orange hues seemed to shine through the breaks in the clouds, but the rain did not stop falling at any moment. I could not understand how such beauty could be obtained on such a dreary day. Yet there I sat looking out the window and witnessing a small sliver of what was to be a majestic and capturing sight.

I nudged Mary slightly on her arm and pointed out the window to which to receive an invigorated moan of pleasure from her when witnessing such a sight.

"Oh Benjamin, it is absolutely gorgeous!" Mary exclaimed.

I could not help but smile at the thought that I had made it possible for her heart to be warmed and her senses pleased. Mary was delighted in the little nuances of life and I could not help but desire to accommodate that need in her. I did not understand her ways at times as our cultures were different, but we both held many similarities when viewing nature. I could not stop myself from watching animals running to and fro while Mary enjoyed the trees and grasses that grew all around. I could see her eyes focusing on such things as if trying to figure out how to capture such elegant beauty on a canvas or in a drawing. She had an eye that beheld vivid colors and represented them so well in her art and I could not wait to see when she would make this move in life again. Mary was a woman of many talents, but her artistic abilities were above reproach when it came to the natural world.

I feared that my wife would fade into this beast and be lost forever if I could not act tomorrow. I no longer had engagements for the next day and I would relish the opportunity to remove Mary from the home. I was not sure that this would help, but if she is not possessed by this dark being then it would go a long way to preventing such things from happening. Surely with such beautiful bonding moments as these, Mary would be showing that she is of sound mind. I felt the urge rising in me to tell her about all that was happening, but I did not wish to impress upon her mind such drastic thoughts.

Any priest would be able to see that Mary had no idea that she could be taken over by such darkness. I could only speculate what a person in that profession might do when seeing a patient as such. It was all that I could do to ponder this until Mary stood from her seat and walked her cup and saucer into the kitchen. I knew that Mary would have to wash the dishes that we had used during the day and return them to the cupboards. Such things were beyond the scope of most men, but I offered to help in any case and was rebuffed. Mary seemed to scoff at the notion and I could not help but I felt that I had overstepped my bounds. I could not see taking such a closely regarded task away from the woman, but I did hope that she would change this opinion in the future.

"You know as well as I, my love, that you shall not touch a dish. I have long enjoyed time in solitude. I have thoughts and reading to entertain me. Just relax here and smoke your pipe until we are ready to retire, my love. Thank you for asking though." Mary stated.

I would not dream of getting involved in something that she would forbid me from doing. It was best that I followed her wishes on the matter and smoked as I normally did during this time of day. What was unexpected was the healthy glass of ice and whiskey placed on the table beside me. A look of amusement and resistance crossed Mary's face as I thanked her for the drink. With this sight, she moved back into the kitchen and began working immediately. I was not sure what reading, of which she had spoken, but I was interested to find out.

Instead, I produced my pipe from my pocket along with some matches and tobacco. It did not take me long to pack the bowl of my pipe and begin striking a match. One swift motion and I had lit the tobacco well while puffing on the mouthpiece to bring about a delicious smoke. I simply sat looking from the front window of our home while puffing away on a whole bowl of tobacco and thinking about the day. Some portions of my day still gave me a crawling sensation on my skin, but I was happy to have survived each situation and had been brought back to peace. I still worried for Mary and her well-being, but these worries were slowly being pushed into the back of my mind. I was simply thankful to have her breathing and healthy on this day with little issues.

I could hear Mary working quickly to finish washing any dishes and placing them in the basin to dry. I knew that she had been drained of energy throughout the day, but I wondered if her sleep last night had not prevented her from truly resting. I had no idea as to how possession would work but the attachment itself would have been a strain on her. I could have asked her directly, but I refused to alarm her when I did not have to do so. Any ideas that I would be able to deposit within Mary's mind might bring about other effects that would not help me assess her situation.

I had never worked in a scientific field, but it was the logical practice of removing doubts about her condition in my mind. I do not wish to look like a fool before the whole world if my wife was not truly ailed by the devil himself. I also did not wish to produce such accusations against Mary and damage her good name. Investigating the way that she felt was only the honorable and right thing to do in our society. My worries and fears could not turn into a blind desire to find something wrong with Mary or her soul. Instead, I shall allow her to do as she will for now, but will be keen about my viewing of her and her interactions. I cannot allow her to fall, but I need more evidence to allow anyone to become involved.

I took a long pull from my pipe again and allowed the smoke to slowly filter out of my mouth. There seemed to be an odd shape forming in the smoke as it floated toward the window. There seemed to be a lot of moisture in the air which should cause the smoke to dissipate rapidly. Instead, it seemed to linger about the window and swirl around as if trying to morph into something else. It seemed that the shape of a shorter woman formed and moved away from me toward the kitchen. I could not see extreme details, but it was enough to know what the form was doing. I could not help but wonder for what purpose and if my mind was strained too much to notice that this was not real. I could see the form round the slight corner into the kitchen and then I heard Mary yell for me. I stood for a moment and called out to her.

"Are you well, Mary? My love, do you need assistance?"

I then moved into the kitchen and looked about the room only to find no one there. Mary seemed to have left in mid-wash, but I did not hear her move at all. We did not live within a quietly built home either as the floor creaked underfoot and would reveal the location of anyone. It was then that I began looking about the room and even toward the ceiling of the room, but saw nothing out of place.

"Where have you gone, my love?" I shouted but no response was offered. There was an instant chill that flowed across my skin and to my feet. I could not help but worry about Mary having left the home in this storm. I checked the front and back doors by standing in the hallway of the lower level. Both doors were shut and did not seem to be disturbed recently.

My next thought was to move up the stairs and check on Mary there, but *why would she move to the upper level?* My instincts were to leave the home and check the street, but I was drawn in an almost dazed feeling toward the upper level. This seemed to flood away, however, once I reached the first step and felt the crunch of the wood moving under my weight. All of my senses came rushing back as I looked up to see Mary suspended in the air and floating toward me with a scream. My heart stopped beating and my blood ran cold as I jumped back. I had no other ideas on how to stop this from happening. I did not wish to make things worse and I would never allow myself to harm Mary in any way.

I then moved to the kitchen and watched for Mary to float her way closer to me. I then spied her changing as she drew nearer to me. She appeared to have aged rapidly as well and I could not see any life within her that I normally would. Her eyes had changed to a reddish-yellow color as she moved toward me. The image made my bones uneasy and my mind ached with the sight. The only thing more terrifying than seeing Mary this way was the horrid scream that she uttered. It was the most terrifying thing that I had ever experienced in my whole existence. I held the spoon higher in my right hand with my left hand free. In no way did I think it would help, but at least I may be able to rescue Mary's mind by confusing her. I could hear nothing but a deep silence in the home. Not even the rain flooded the area with a light sound as if something were blocking the sounds altogether.

I gently moved forward toward the opening that lead to the dining room then peaked out for a momentary glance. I could neither see nor feel anyone standing near the opening as if waiting for me. I could feel sweat beginning to form on my head and neck, but I had no choice but to shrug it off. I knew that if Mary found me before I found her then I would be attacked without knowing what to do. I continued through the dining room and looked down the short hallway toward the stairs.

I could see nothing, however, as I felt the sudden cold chill that washed through the space. I checked every corner as I moved forward slowly, but I could find nothing out of place or Mary. The sitting room and back hallway seemed to be the same empty space as the rest of the home. I could not feel that Mary would have left as both doors, once again, were as if they had never been touched. This was most perplexing, to say the least, but I knew that she would haunt me once more if I moved closer to the stairs themselves. It was then that I froze in place feeling the sweat beginning to run down my face.

I could hear the footsteps pacing across the floors above me and my heart responded with a loud beating. My hearing was flooded with a buzzing sound as my heart beat faster and faster within my chest. Without warning, the steps moved to just above me and then stopped completely. What would she be doing in our room and how could she be standing directly above me in such a way? If my memory served me, she would be standing in the middle of our bed closer to that wall. Nothing made sense to my rational self, but it had to end before harm came to Mary or myself. Just then a shrieking bellowed from the upper floor as Mary began screaming like a banshee. The sound was deafening as my head began pounding with pain and I fell to the floor. My vision blurred more with each passing moment and I could not be sure whether she was still screaming or if my mind had simply been infected with that horrible sound.

My heart began fluttering uneasily then everything went dark again. I had not lost consciousness but, rather, found myself unable to think, hear or see. Any and all attempts to close my eyes and open them did nothing at first, but then a blurry vision began flooding my mind. Several men entered our home through the door and moved up the stairs of the home. It was then that the man from the train, Mr. Edgar, moved to me and pulled me into the dining room. I felt him lower me into a chair as my vision faded in and out until I felt and heard nothing. I had finally lost consciousness again, but it was like my mind had been erased as when I came about, I was sitting in a chair being nudged by an officer.

"Are you all right sir? Hello?" He spoke. "I think this one is a bit drunk...get her out of here and into the wagon. I'll make sure this one sobers up."

I pushed toward the officer upon hearing them taking Mary away, but I could do nothing. I simply stood in a forward rushing move, but collided with the officer and fell to the ground in my weakness.

"Sir, don't move if you can. Here...help me with him" the officer said.

I could hear a slight grunt from both men as they struggled against me to place me back into the chair from which I had launched myself.

"Are you coherent sir? Can you hear me?"

I did not know enough to respond, but I could hear myself muttering faint commands to the officers. *"No, bring her back! Don't take Mary away! My Mary!", y*et I could do nothing at all to stop this from happening. My arms and legs were not stable in any way and my vision, though recovering, was still blurry.

It was then that I could hear the worst sounds imaginable as the wagon began driving away from our home as Mary continued to beg and scream from the wagon. It was then that my mind rushed with an anger that I had not felt in some time. It was as though something had awoken within my soul as I stood from the chair and pushed past the officers as though they were children. I launched into the streets and ran after the wagon as I removed my coat and threw it on the ground. My top hat simply flew from my head until I reached the vehicle.

I pulled myself onto the back of the wagon to see Mary sitting in the darkness with her hair drenched from the rain. I found it hard to keep my grasp on the amount of water that flowed across the iron bars.

"Do not worry my love. I will find where they are taking you and remove you from that place!" I exclaimed.

The only response that I received was that of a cackle that emanated from within the wagon and a force that pulled at my shirt. I was removed from the back of the wagon and dragged to the ground by another officer. He was a larger sort of fellow and immediately lifted me to my feet with ease.

"I am sorry about that sir. She will be cared for and safe. We are just taking her to Witherbrook Asylum and she will be checked in with the desk. Come by in the morning to see her there. Once again I am sorry, sir, but you must return home and rest from your ordeal."

He then handed me my hat and coat which were now drenched in water from all of the rain that fell upon the ground. With those words, he turned and began walking in the direction of a horse then rode off to follow the wagon. I had heard of this Witherbrook and I knew little of it. Surely Mary would be protected by God in such a place until morning. At this point, I could do nothing but pray for her soul and safety, but I felt so useless. A quiet rage built within my mind and heart as everything began to sink in.

I would not stand for this insult at the hands of this evil beast. I would no longer allow myself to be prey to this nor Mary. It was time to move forward with the defense of my life and my home. I cared no longer for how I would appear within society as it was now my home that had been torn asunder. It did not take me long to move back to my home and place my coat and hat on the first chair in the sitting room to dry. I grasped my gun from the table and holstered it once again, but in plain sight as I no longer wore my coat. I heard the door slam shut behind me as I hailed a coach to take me to Edric's. Time blurred together into a streak of thought until I reached Edric's street. It was as if a switch flipped within my mind as I was instantly brought back into my senses and I could feel hate. Pure hate flowed in my veins with every thought of Mary being taken from me. *Who had called for the officers? Was this enigmatic Edgar figure truly within my home?* My mind raced with these thoughts until I stepped from the coach and onto the street. I handed the driver a tip and moved quickly to Edric's door.

I had become so enraged, in fact, that I could not feel my flesh slapping against the hearty wooden door of his home. I simply beat the door as I wished and could feel it giving way slightly with each hit. I did not wish to be disrespectful to Edric or the sanctity of his home, but I needed these answers now.

6

E dric opened the door with confusion scattered across his face. "Benjamin? Are you well sir? Come in!" He stated.

I wasted no time entering his home just to exclaim, "They took Mary, Edric! I believe she is possessed and I will not stand for this! This demon is going to be banished one way or another!"

Edric seemed stunned as I yelled this out, but said nothing. He simply held out a glass of whiskey which I took swiftly and swallowed in one gulp. He could feel my rage and replied, "Calm yourself, Benjamin. What in God's name has happened?"

I told him the events that had just transpired as he bid me follow him deeper within his home.

Edric then took me into the back portion of his study which was a room that was, amazingly, empty. He then moved something within a darkened corner to produce the sounds of a latch being opened. Edric then walked to the middle of the floor and rolled a rug back to reveal a door in the flooring which he then lifted. This revealed stairs that faded slowly into the darkness below. Only dim light filtered into this space as Edric began walking into the darkness. He then removed a lantern from an alcove in the wall and lit it in a rather calm manner.

"Follow me. We will find out what is happening with your wife."

I did nothing but rattle off my story of all that had happened to this point without losing any details. Edric said nothing at first, but simply leaned with his leg crossed over the other against the wall of the stairs. He then waved his hand forward as we moved into a room that looked like a mausoleum with a low ceiling. He then began lighting torches that had been placed around the room only to reveal rows and rows of lower bookshelves. Each book seemed much older than anything I had ever known. The whole of the room seemed more like a setting from a fantasy tale about knights and wizards. I was taken by surprise by this sight as my anger swiftly flooded away from me. Edric moved to the furthest point within the space and lit two hanging braziers which lit the area with a dim but full light. It was not the flicker of a candle, but a constant light that seemed to shine within the space without being enough to see everything. Edric then approached me again after having removed a book from a far shelf and placed it on one of the two long tables in the middle of the room.

Edric placed it gently on the table then opened it to a random page and pointed out a mural on the opposite page. It was of a grotesque creature that seemed to be otherworldly in every way. It was a tall being with tentacles about its face and seemed to be the ruler of some oceanic depths, but I did not recognize it or its form. I simply shook my head and Edric began moving to the next section of the book that he wished to highlight. This section began with a mural that appeared to be the same empty void that I had witnessed before me on the train. I could not help but think back to this vision once more yet I did not wish to be pulled into this void again. Edric furrowed his brow at the sight of my face upon my remembrance of this event. I could see that Edric wished to ask me what I had witnessed but he would not out of reverence for my torment.

"This is an interesting section within this book. It is based upon the works of John Dee who set down interesting formations about such a place in the sixteenth century. I could not begin to understand such an existence, but the void appears to be very real within the afterlife or para-existence. In some understandings about such things, others would have to equate this to the belief in purgatory within the Catholic faith, but it is a much more unsettling place."

Edric turned to the next page and pointed out a section of these writings.

"I will tell you that Mr. Dee had never expressly described this place in detail, but this tome has been compiled in the seventeenth century and uses John Dee's works to make sense of his occult knowledge. The being that you are being haunted by would be a horrid thing. It is not supposed to be within our realm, but you will have some connection with it through family lines. Do you know how this being would have been summoned and when?"

I could not understand how Edric would have known such things, but I did not possess this book nor the knowledge that it contained so I would have to take him at his word. I had never known Edric to lie to anyone nor would he have been able to make such details up without a lot of time invested in this lie. I could not stop myself from uttering:

"My aunt and mother have summoned such a creature. I remember the visions that I had upon arriving in North Carolina. They were horrible Edric, but I cannot help but think that they would have had a reason to do this. Yet all intellect would be baffled as to why I would have witnessed such things from a past time."

Edric said nothing at first, he stared off into the dark and damp corner of the room as he rubbed his chin in thought. I could see that he had started putting pieces into this complicated puzzle the more he pondered it.

"This would all be signs of something that I have only understood within the literature that I would have thought is fiction. Surely it cannot be real, but again I would say that you are being slowly pulled closer to the void. Yes...the void shall find you if you do not stop this being and soon. I am sorry my friend, but how have you been keeping this being at bay?"

I tilted my head slightly toward the right as I could not understand such a question.

"I have done nothing. This is why I have come to you Edric. I need guidance on how to remove such things from my life."

Edric nodded then closed the tome and walked back toward the place of origin for the book.

"There is nothing that you can do to remove this being from your life unless you're able to defeat the thing yourself. This is something that I can only speculate upon, but it seems that this 'demon' as you would call it is nothing more than a ghost. That is to say that it can only influence you, but possession is more than likely. Slowly, you will notice that this being will become more and more physical, but it is only able to be defeated by robbing it of its anchor to this world."

"Would this happen to be a home or something within a home, that when burned would remove this entity from its anchor?" I asked.

Edric nodded quickly and then replied, "Yes. This would be possible. As long as this place or thing was destroyed then there would be no way for this being to be held by its anchor. You can know the anchor by the place in which these rituals were performed to bring this being to our world. Once this step is completed then it is a waiting game as this being will begin to solidify within our world and try to become a physical being, but can attack you within dreams or possess you."

Instantly my mind began to race with thoughts about Mary's possible possession. This being could not attack me with any satisfaction but needed someone to reach me with desperation and fear as if showing some control over my life. It now became clear to me that this being had become desperate to instill fear or something akin to worry within my mind to bring itself into reality.

"This being will seek to form an attachment with your emotions to feed off of any negative nature within your life. I would say that this being would begin tormenting those who had summoned it to bring about any sustenance that it would need to form into a being other than a spirit. Now it has no anchor and will begin to haunt someone then transform into a much more traditional demonic infestation."

"How would I be able to take this power from this being?" I asked. Edric thought for a moment as he brought another tome over to the table. He then moved to another bookcase and brought a candle to the table then motioned for me to take my place at this table.

"This book outlines such beings that are not light nor dark. They are entities known as something like a *djinn* or a *maw*-like creature. Though this being does not inhabit our world or realm in the least. They are just as the Bible would describe the evils of Satan, but they are not demons of the pits of hell. This is something different and hungry for life. They are waiting just beyond this world, always looking into our realm and waiting for the right time. It is like walking past a mirror and seeing someone else looking back from the corner of your eye. These beings always use portals like mirrors or windows to look within our world. Cover any mirrors that you possess and never call to anyone through the window while this being haunts you."

I could have never imagined such happenings within my logical mind, but I have witnessed many odd things in my life since arriving in North Carolina.

"How can one hurt such a being Edric?"

He thought for a moment and then began looking through the book, "It is outlined that the normal items that hurt spirits will hurt such a being. Iron, salt, the smoke of sage, and certain fragrances that have been imported from the Orient. I would be cautious to remember that the objective is to take anyone connected to those who would have summoned such a being into the void from which it has come. It would be done at the request of the summoner and I would wager that this deal would be made without knowing that someone is with a child or a husband or lover could be offered as payment."

Edric's words were alarming, to say the least, and I could not help but put the puzzle to these recent happenings together in my mind. I knew now that my suspicions had been given life within this conversation with Edric. My mother and aunt could have to have offered my life and the life of my father without knowing that she would be able to even have a child. I was not sure which angered me more, the thought that she would offer my father in such a way or myself before I was even imagined. *Was it that she would take me along to North Carolina on her visits to my aunt to assist this entity in taking me to the void? How careless could my mother have been in such an instance?* I could not begin to understand how she would have reached the thoughts needed to ensure that she would be able to sacrifice her only child.

Edric closed the tome on the table, "Do not blame your mother for this. The entity would relish this opportunity as it makes you weaker, and less focused. We cannot fall into this thinking around such a coercive entity."

"What do you mean we?" I asked quickly.

Edric stood in a bold fashion and pushed his chest out as if joining some legendary mission, "I am coming with you, Benjamin. You need help and I know that Mary has been taken away. She needs us to protect and help her. Otherwise, she will perish along with yourself."

This was a bold statement, but nothing could be more of the truth. I knew that Edric had supported such things in thought, but he had never offered his assistance like this before. Typically it was his fashion to simply offer knowledge on a subject or process rather than become directly embroiled. I was fortunate, however, that he would even offer to help me in such a way. I could never understand why he would wish this upon himself while still knowing the pain and suffering that will accompany such an offer.

I thanked him and departed his home for the night with the instructions that we would meet in the morning at Edric's home. He also gave me a small piece of paper with instructions on protections for myself until we could meet. I closed the door behind me with a thud and wondered once more into the rain-filled night. I could hear the drops of rain pounding against the brick and concrete within the streets of the city as if thousands of hands slapping against a stone.

My hat had been sloppily placed upon my head while I dared not place my rain-soaked coat upon my back for fear of sickness.

I could feel my heart beating faster and faster while my mind seemed to race with thought after thought about how to return Mary to our usual life. My heart tortured me with fears of what might be done to Mary until the morning. I thought of taking a route to the asylum, but I know in my heart that I would be turned away. I longed for Mary's touch again and her words of love and comfort, but I could not linger upon these emotions without feeling a surge of sadness and misery begin to wash over me. Instead, I approached the street over from my home while trying to not focus on the night wanderers. These were the people that I had no intention of entertaining or mingling with as I was not that sort of man. In my youth, I had taken many a night by storm and drank my fill in the company of many a woman. Now I did not wish for such things as Mary and I were meant to have a peaceful and wholesome life without such temptations haunting us.I walked along the street until I had reached my home and then slowly unlocked the door. I pushed it open with a low creaking from the hinges pulling against the wood and frame. I looked back only to notice that the lock had transformed into a hand that pulled against me until I had begun to slide out of the doorway slightly. I pulled against it with all my might, but I could not force this apparition to release me. It was then that this feeling of peace and righteous anger came over me as I placed my hand over the one that grasped me. I called out to God with a command to release this being from my life to plague me no more. The lock shifted its form once again back to a lock as I nodded and said, "right!", then closed the door. I no longer cared for this being or its torments within my home and life. I had reached exhaustion and contempt for such things as I could feel no fear for this being nor its attempts to drag me into it.

I wasted no time in producing a bottle of scotch from the kitchen only to begin drowning my emotions. Gulp after gulp passed my lips until I could feel the world beginning to darken both within my home and outside the door. Each swig of the bottle brought me closer to the floor and into a delirious state that I could no longer control. I had no desire to linger within this trance, however, as I would begin preparing my materials tonight. I would desire the blood of this being if indeed it had any within its body. I wanted this being to feel the torment that had befallen Mary and myself. I moved to the dining room table and unpinned the doors on each side of the room to seal me away from the rest of the home. I then produced salt and crimping devices from the kitchen as I kept tools within the kitchen space.

I then began working on salt charges and 'sanctified bullets' immediately as laid out by Edric. It involved praying over a bowl of water while placing the lead bullets within the liquid for some time. Once this is done, you immediately mix salt within the powder behind the bullet until you pack everything back into the shell then load the gun. Salt charges are a bit tricky as they involve making an improvised explosive pack that spreads sale upon anything that is in the area. I modified the charge recipe and packed some sage within the charge along with the salt to give a more even spread and create much more interaction with any entity that it hit. The sage was as pure as I could use from our herb garden in the back of our home. Some of this called for silver to be used as I would produce a fire within the old, iron stove in the kitchen after struggling to pull it out from the wall.

I placed a small bundle of silverware into an iron pot and then started an intense fire inside the stove. I produced a bellow from the rear storage room just across the hallway from the kitchen. I then blew it into a small pipe that had been used as a handle for the fire door on the side of the stove. When positioned right, this gave the right amount of airflow into the fire contained within the core of the stove and gave life to such a powerful flame. Once the wood had begun to glow, I mixed a coal compound into the flame and began pumping the bellows vigorously until it had reached the relative temperature that I needed. The Iron had begun glowing with the heat that had been produced from the flames. I placed the iron pot filled with silverware into the flame and covered it with the coals.

I continued in this way until the silver had melted into a very even liquid within the pot. With this, I removed the pot and placed it on the top of the stove to begin a slight cooling as I crimped the silver into the shape of a ball. This was then prayed over and placed upon the surface once solidifying had begun. The shot that had been produced was not refined in any way as this was a crude process, to say the least, but it provided much in the way of protection. The only thing left to accomplish was to salt the doorway to my bedroom. Yet I held my place within the kitchen as the stove cooled. I finished the bottle of scotch and moved on to a good, American, aged whiskey.

I drank my fill until I did not remember falling into a deep sleep on the kitchen floor. It was the only thing that stopped my heart from waking me in misery as my wife could no longer be found within our home. It seemed out of place to sleep in our bed as no one would occupy it with me. The warmth and life of our home had now faded and it seemed that I would no longer be able to live with any cohesion once again, but it was this chaos that bore my inquisitive nature. Now I would use this opportunity to bring about diligence and resolve within this lifestyle then hammer my psyche back together with the determination of killing this demon.

I had every intention to banish this being back to the void that bore it into our realm and then spit upon its memory. I was the son of a soldier and belonged to a family that would reach for great ends to accomplish what it desired. By this very nature, this being would meet its end within our world and I would be reunited with my loving wife again. I would never rest until I could have Mary to myself once more while being able to move past everything happening now.

My mind raced with thoughts that I had never understood to be present and it seemed that I had been awakened in spirit but my mind and body rested upon the ground. I could see all around me, but not with the clarity that I had known in my physical eyes. It seemed that this version of my reality had become more real with each passing visit as my spirit felt the lingering cold of this realm. I was as alone as I had ever been, but I felt none of the worries or fears associated with this. Instead, I began journeying through this dim realm with a light that seemed to emanate from within my soul.

I could hear rain slamming into the ground outside my home along with the feeling of being watched from every corner. I stepped out of the rear hallway and looked into the entryway of my home only to see a woman standing in the corner to the left of the front door. I did not dare call out to her as I knew this would bring about a fresh sort of horror. Instead, I slowly approached her whilst checking all around me. I knew that anything could startle me at this moment and I would not have the physical world to protect me. I felt as though I was adrift within an alien ocean to which I did not belong yet. Death was a realm in which I held no power, but this was the void between the world. I relegated my safety to my body, however, as I kept my mind focused on my sleeping self. It was then that I realized that I was not holding a light within my form but in my hand as I held a lantern further in front of myself to see more clearly.

Now I had begun to slip up behind this being as it continued to stand motionless in the corner of the entryway. I made no sound as I reached out for the woman, but before I could make contact with her shoulder, she began to sob which gave me pause. This was an intense crying that seemed to start suddenly, but she did not move to cover her face. I reached further still and placed a finger upon her until I heard,

"This will be your last Benjamin!" She whispered. I pulled my hand back to myself instantly as she turned suddenly and screamed. Blood had begun pouring from her mouth and eyes as she opened both wide until all that could be visible was a bloody void from which a screaming emerged.

I jumped back faster than I had ever in my life only to see that this was my mother. She had a younger form that I had never witnessed save for photos of her. She crouched slightly with clawed hands resting on each side of her then she began slowly approaching me.

"Make no further moves, Mother. You have no reason to torment the son that you wished away before ever knowing! You do not protest love upon selling a soul that is not yours!" I exclaimed.

This did nothing to change her course as laughter could be heard now instead of screaming. I could feel my soul beginning to move slowly back as she approached closer and closer.

"I wish your torment away from my life, Mother! Take leave of me now!"

Still, nothing changed as she continued slowly as I chose to move away from her form and began moving toward the stairs. She then began sprinting toward me while scratching her clawed hand across the walls. I could hear the sounds of her torment flowing forth from all directions until I yelled,

"No longer torment my heart, vile woman! You chose this bed and it will not torment me any longer!"

I had closed my eyes once I had begun yelling only to open them again to see that my mother was gone. I held out my lantern once more to see if she had another form in store for me, but I could see nothing. Only darkness lingered beyond my lantern and the flickering flame that it held. The world around me seemed coated in a green, sickly hue that covered everything. I knew not if this was the end for my soul, but I felt compelled to journey onward deeper into my home.

I gently moved up the stairs to the second level and began peeking into the spare bedroom to my left. I could see a large darkened form that was hunched in the far corner once more. It made no movement and no reaction to anything that I could do as I could feel that it knew I had arrived. I slowly and quietly made the move toward the bedroom as I tried to avoid this being at all costs. I could never be sure, but I could understand that this was the being that haunted my life and my bloodline. I did not wish to attract its attention nor be attacked by it in this weakened state as something felt awry in this darkened plane. I continued to walk back until I collided with what I thought was the door to my bedroom, but it was not. I turned only to see a bricked-up opening as I could not feel a doorknob or frame. I panicked at that moment and began pressing against the brick in desperation to escape.

It was then that I could hear the boards of this home creaking and flexing as though under great stress. I froze in place, refusing to turn around as I knew that I had attracted this beast. I could not understand what had happened or whether this being had conjured this wall to stop me from escaping. I took a deep breath in only to taste the sickly, sweet flavors of this realm. It was a gentle rot that seemed to assault the senses and steal the peace from any mind that would attempt to contemplate such realms. I looked over my shoulder slowly to see this form standing behind me, but at what distance, I could not tell.

I then turned to see that it was a hulking thing in the middle of the room in which I had found it. I tried to not make any movement as I was not sure that this being would strike out or chase me, but I knew that I could not stop anything that it would attempt. My being knew that the only way to stop this entity was to reunite with my body once again and remove my spirit from its path. This would raise issues in it trying to influence the physical realm to kill or harm me in any way. I would then have the upper hand in defending against its evil and malice toward my life.

I immediately made a dash for the steps and began leaping down them until I had reached the bottom then leaped over the last set of steps to the ground. Once I had turned to move down the small hallway just off the kitchen, I could see that it had expanded and seemed to do so the further that I ran. In an instant, it all moved closer to me in a rush of wind and confusion, I was knocked to the ground as I could hear movement behind me. I looked back toward the stairs to see this entity crawling slowly and deliberately across the ceiling of the lower level. I could hardly believe my eyes until the creature seemed to approach my position as if a cat toying with a mouse.

I panicked and rolled onto my feet only to spring forward and into the kitchen, but I could see no end in sight. My body had vanished completely from the kitchen while leaving no clues as to where it had gone. *Where had my body gone? What had happened to me while being trapped here?* I saw nothing indicating that my body had or could move independently of my soul, but it was gone. I looked back out of the kitchen only to see this being rushing toward my location and had now changed to swimming through the structure of the walls as a fish in the ocean. I could not understand this at all, but I brought my focus back to the task at hand and rushed out of the other door and into the dining room. Everything levitated and seemed to become an obstacle as the floor fell away.

Now there was nothing on which to place my weight save for the floating table and chairs. Once more, I could feel this being approaching quickly as I leaped out and pulled myself onto the seat of a chair. With one thrust of my arms upward and a slight jump, I had begun to mount the table and climb atop. I turned to see this being stalled at the entrance to the room but clearly changing its strategy for how to stop my escape from this wretched place. I did not wish to wait any longer as I raced across the table and jumped from its edge. I landed upon another seat of a chair with a thud while having to steady my balance again to avoid falling away from this platform. This being had now vanished from the place where it once stood and all sound flooded away. I again held out the lantern and looked all around the floating chair to the darkened and empty floor below.

It was then that I could see this being swimming toward me through the floor like a monstrous serpent moving through an ocean within a cave. As such I could see nothing clearly and had become much more confused with approaching this new change in this game. I then watched as the table and other chairs fell upon the surface of this blackened water and then began to dissolve as if melting into the void that was the floor. My heart jumped in my chest and my veins ran cold at witnessing such a sight. I wasted no more time and jumped with all my intention and might into the entryway to the home as I hoped that I would be able to land safely on solid ground. I closed my eyes tightly until the soles of my boots landed upon the firm flooring with a loud clopping sound. I opened my eyes slowly and began looking all around me as I noticed that everything had changed from the typical home that I had come to know.

Nothing seemed out of place in the least and I had begun to think that I had been reunited with my body and thrust into the physical realm once again. It was now that I could see a light beginning to shine in the distance. It was beautiful and radiant as it slowly grew brighter in this darkened world. I moved my arm to shield my eyes until the light formed into a shape that coalesced into the curvy form of a beautiful female. It was then that I could hear Mary's voice and I collapsed to the ground. My love, my wife, she had returned to me once again to make things right once more. I could not help but wonder if this meant that she had passed on from this realm, but I could not speak.

"It has your body within our room, my love. You must go now to return. I am safe here and it has my body. Free me, my love. Please go now!" Mary exclaimed.

I could not find the strength in my legs to get to my feet until I saw the entity wrapping itself around Mary and grasping her soul by its neck. I could see Mary's spirit weakening slowly with this grasp, but I could do nothing. The rage and hate tempered within my soul as I desired this being's complete destruction. I knew that this would be the outcome to get Mary back, but I had to leave as I had been told. No matter the desires that I felt within, I could never stop this being within this realm. I forced myself back to my feet as the world began to shake and contort. Tendrils began emerging from the walls and floors as I approached and began climbing the stairs to the upper level. I ducked under the tendrils that launched themselves forth from the walls as I ran up the steps to the upper landing. It was then that I balanced myself on the edge of the upper landing due to one last tendril lashing out and smashing through the brick wall that separated me from my room.

I ran toward the wall and launched myself through the new opening, landing on my bed. I could feel the world shift once more and everything fell away to reveal my body sitting in the corner of the bedroom as I launched myself forward and smashed into my physical form. Instantly I opened my eyes and took a deep breath as I had begun to cough in a groggy stupor. I could not understand all that had happened within my brain but I knew the ordeal was real as I could feel the exhaustion coursing through me.

The only reaction that I could muster now was to swill down the rest of the bottle and then remove myself from the floor. I could see nothing wrong with the world now but I still felt the all-consuming anger that burned within my heart. Tomorrow would be a reckoning for these beings that had taken Mary. I would not take this attack upon my life and my love lying down for any reason. I climbed onto the bed and fell asleep on my comfortable sheets without any more incidents. The world faded to a deepened black as I had fallen asleep and began moving forward through time.

7

The morning broke through the bedroom window as I opened my sleepy eyes. Groggy was not the word to describe how I felt, but exhausted and drained of all energy seemed more accurate. I could not hear any thought that seemed to be moving through my mind nor could I understand much. I had fallen into a horrible state since drinking so much the night before. I moved slowly from my place in the middle of the mattress and began dressing. I wish that I could say that this was within my normal capabilities to operate at an optimal level, but I would be lying. My mind and my body seemed to no longer communicate together but in some ways better than before.

No longer would I second guess my decisions whilst in this state, but reaction without consideration, in this case, seemed to be more powerful. Perhaps it was that I had become my father's son and appreciated the drink a little too much. As I returned to focus, I found myself gazing out the window at a small and beautiful bird that seemed to have no cares in the world. I tied my ascot and straightened my suit coat without moving my gaze away from this innocent creature. I had become captivated by the beauty and gentle nature of such a being as it reminded me of why I was doing what I was about to do.

Now it was the case that the sun had only begun to glint through the world as I shut my front door and turned the lock to shut up my home from anyone else. I then strolled to the street and hailed a coach to take me to Edric's home. I was sure that he would be prepared as well and ready for the fight that we would engage ourselves in on this day. I could not understand how he would have known about such things without being engaged in this activity before. Surely both of us were not walking into a foreign world without any knowledge of what might happen. This thought concerned me little, however, as I did not fear this being any longer. Instead, I held a steely focus on the world and all that happened around me.

I could not be certain as to why or how, but I was sure that I would find these answers during the conflict with the otherworldly. I had only these thoughts upon my mind as I exited the coach and was greeted by Edric from the door of his home. I hurried through his door and into the foyer as quickly as I could then removed my coat and placed it upon his coat rack in the entryway.

"Are you prepared for our adventure today?"

I nodded without hesitation.

"I am ready for anything that could be brought against us. How have you fared, Edric?" I asked.

"I am well, Master Benjamin. I assure you that this is not the first time that I have engaged in such things. Though, never in such a public venue as an asylum. I did take the liberty of having a look over some blueprints to Witherbrook that a friend provided me. It is as good a place as any to move about without being seen as our guns are drawn. Half of the grounds have been left in a state, but still sprawling and empty. If there are to be any engagements with such an evil, we will have to do it there to prevent harm to anyone else."

Edric motioned for me to move further into his home and presented some small rations upon the counter.

"Eat now as we may not get the chance to do so later. I am sure that this place will not roll out a seven-course meal for us." Edric stated with confidence in his voice.

We both laughed at such a thought and then prepared our equipment and selves for the departure. This was done with care to not disturb anything that we would carry with us and while eating some of the rations that had been hastily prepared. It was not the best meal that I had ingested in my life, but not the worst. It was better than hard bread and much more filling than water.

"We only have one chance to take Mary from her room to perform the ritual needed. You will have to do the talking and introduce me as someone who is assisting your home. Surely we will be able to remove her without much question, but we will have to be cautious anyway. Also, Mary may lash out against us both. Be careful Benjamin! I cannot tell you how important it is to be cautious."

I simply nodded my head as we both placed our hats upon our heads and then left Edric's home. Witherbrook was some distance away by boat, but we had to take care to be there promptly. Edric hailed a coach and we were off on our journey to the asylum. I feared for Mary's safety since her departure the evening of the previous day, but I knew that she was in God's hands at this point. Surely this demon would never allow any excessive harm to come to its vessel in the interim.

I asked questions about such things to Edric, but he simply deflected these questions in favor of a blank stare. Eventually, I gathered that he would not know such things or that the answers would be too hard for my mind to understand. I simply stopped asking questions as Edric began reaching out to feel the air around the coach as we approached the docks and the waterfront. I did not understand this nor his silence during any conversation that we might have, but I put it down to concentration and mental preparation for the coming battle.

Time passed slowly as we rode to the docks and then were let out upon the boardwalk that led to the fairy loading area. I could see that a few men worked around the boat and had set out the gangplank to board the vessel, but were not observant enough to see Edric and me as we approached. My mind had begun racing with nervous resolve, but hunger for justice to be done to Mary. I had no idea how or where we would travel upon the island on which Witherbrook rested or where we would find our secluded place to remove this entity from her soul, but I left it all up to Edric.

I stepped out of the coach following Edric as I had begun to notice that a thick and relentless fog had rolled into the area. Not a moment before, the sky had been dim as the sun peeked above the horizon, but visibility was ample. Now it seemed that we had moved into a fog-ridden swamp that appeared to be allied against our journey. We could both hear the faint sounds of water washing back and forth from below the docks, but could still see nothing at all. There was a perceived sound of people walking back and forth across the deck of a ship, but no other sounds could be heard. These factors were enough to cause Edric and me a slight reluctance and desire to protect ourselves from a perceived threat.

Though the morning was still in its beginning stages, I would have expected there to be more workers moving about the docks and preparing the Ferry to launch out across the waters around the city. Yet Edric and I moved toward the gangplank and up onto the vessel before us without pause or pulling notice. We were then greeted by a man dressed as a boatman who seemed to materialize from the fog before us.

"Mornin' to ya sirs! The fog is a bit thick eh?" He stated and followed with a hearty laugh. "It doesn't matt'ah, however, we are about to get underway. Have a seat if you will or stand about!"

Edric and I never responded formally but shook the man's hand and nodded to him in acknowledgment of his words then watched as he faded away as quickly as he had appeared. I then followed Edric to the front of the boat as we both gazed out over the water that was not visible from the fog. Surely it would not be possible for our boat to launch under these conditions, but I would place my trust upon the captain's shoulders. The only presence that would matter now would be that of my courage rising to the occasion against these insurmountable odds. I had to muster all of the inner diligence that I could to save Mary from this destructive fate. Nothing would be a better decision in the least and I could never understand how it would feel to be taken by such an entity as my hope of being saved wanes.

This was my individual responsibility to my wife and my family to the point that it had become a personal crusade of a sort. If Edric or I were to fail in our call to action against such a being, Mary would be lost completely to the darkness that threatened our peace. Even with these acknowledgments, I still thought that my mind had reached the edge of sanity and reason. I could only feel what my heart would tell me within this moment, which was to never return home without Mary in hand. Edric stood silently just a small distance away from me and stared into the fog as the rotation of the ship paddles started to increase in revolutions. I could now feel myself being pulled back slightly as we began moving forward and away from the dock.

Edric, the captain, and I would now be at the mercy of weather and time. The sounds of the waves sloshing against the side of the boat as we moved forward and toward the left seemed to increase as the sound of each rotation of the paddles became increasingly louder. It was then that I noticed that the fog had begun to break ahead of us slowly but surely. Perhaps it was that the fog would instill a sense of caution in us from the beginning rather than inhibiting our ability to reach the island that was our target. Then came the piercing sound of a horn blaring into the world around us which startled me.

I could only consider the thoughts of my lovely wife with limited presence in my mind as I dared not allow myself to fall into a loss of motivation or misery. Instead, my heart burned with defiant anger that would not leave me in peace. I was determined; emboldened to bring justice to this situation without wavering. My mind could have no room for a loss in desire for a resolution by any means that was necessary. Even if it meant the death of Mary in her fragile state, I did desire for this to not be the outcome. I had grown to accept this outcome simply for the sake of preparing my heart and self for the misery that was inevitable to follow such an event.

I could not feel that the wind had whipped up around the boat and across the deck as my outer coat had begun floating in the wind with the occasional slapping against the back of my ankles. The chill that traveled with this unsettled air seemed to reach my bones without regard for how it would affect my mood. I still stood stoic against the scene as the fog finally broke its hold on our ship and we moved toward the now visible island. The whole of the asylum seemed to be wrapped in a mysterious wreath of fog and rushing air. It appeared as if the elemental of air had grasped hold of the structure and threatened to crush it to nothing. It was now that Edric turned to me:

"We must focus our minds now, Benjamin! We cannot allow our hearts to get the best of our minds if we are to save your wife. Steel yourself from fear and doubt, for this is the day that the Lord hath made! Now check your weapons and equipment. We don't want to show that we are armed when entering this facility. We will likely be rebuffed from entry and I don't want to have to kidnap Mary from the state to accomplish our goals."

I nodded to Edric and immediately began checking the charges and ammunition that I had crafted the night before. This was all followed by checking my pistol and silver rod for any issues or jams. With a fluid spin of the cylinder, I could feel a well-oiled and balanced mechanism that was sure to not fail me in a time of need. I had come to rely upon this mechanical operation to protect myself when there was no other solution for personal safety.

Within moments Edric and I departed the boat and stepped onto the dock without any other guidance. Yet we could see a faint light approaching us from the other end of the dock in a slow and swinging manner. Just then wind whipped up from under the dock as a moaning sound could be heard in the distance. Immediately after this, a man emerged from the fog with his lantern held before him and beckoned us to follow him. Neither of us heard anything that he would have spoken as instruction, but we knew that he must be the doorman of the asylum. It was custom to guide anyone who would visit the asylum to the door in ailing weather.

Even with such guidance Edric and I were on edge, to say the least, as we began approaching the building itself. We continued to keep an eye on each other as well to not lose sight of each other in such thick fog, yet we reached the door nonetheless. The doorman paused and turned to Edric and me with his hand resting upon the oversized handle of the door.

"Sirs, please enter carefully. Something has served a dark purpose here and the fools are overly excited." He stated.

I could hear the sorrow and worry in his voice as we were let into the lobby of the asylum, but I could not understand his reason for saying it until the doors were closed and the howling of the winds had been diminished. Before us stood a woman squar behind a desk who seemed to be unsurprised that we had arrived.

"Names, sirs?" She asked in a monotone voice.

We both answered the woman and provided our reason for our visit as seeing my wife and Edric had arrived for support.

"Yes. She is just down the hall then turn the corner. The door is on your left."

This was the last that this woman had spoken to Edric and myself before we nodded and thanked her for the help. It did not take us long to round the corner and stand in front of Mary's room, but something seemed off as we opened the door and peered in. Mary was crouched in the far corner behind the bed and seemed lost in every way. She muttered something to herself and began twitching slightly, but then her strange actions and words seemed to start over as if she were stuck in a loop. The display was odd, to say the least, and I could feel myself being taken off guard by such an odd sighting. Edric did not seem to share the same pause as he moved into the room and began trying to receive any reaction from Mary at all.

"Mary? Are you all right? Has God taken you into his court?" Edric asked.

I found this line of questioning to be odd and unsettling, but there arose an immediate response. A growl emanated from Mary's person toward Edric then changed to a low murmur. Then Mary began the eerie loop of behavior once more without regarding us further.

"How shall we remove my wife from this wretched place? There are no windows in here and we cannot take her out the front door."

Edric stopped for a moment and thought without even looking in my direction. I could feel that he was conflicted about the best method for removing her. The fog itself would provide the cover needed for us to move to a more remote building on the island, but I was not sure where that would be since I could not see any other structures on the island. Without much more thought, Edric pulled the sheets from Mary's bed and began wrapping her in them as she fought against him, though her attempts to fight back were weak in any regard.

He then looked toward me as if he expected me to know how and where to remove ourselves from the main asylum building. Immediately I leaned from the doorway and looked up and down the hallway only to find that there was one window at the other end. I motioned to Edric to follow as we moved down the hallway and reached the window. The air outside had begun swirling and the sky darkened rapidly as if a sudden storm had begun forming over the island. I felt along the bottom of the window until I slipped my fingers under the wooden frame and slipped the latch back then lifted the window slowly.

It did not take long for Edric to move through the window then followed by removing Mary through the same portal and slipping into the woods just beyond. I followed swiftly and lowered the window back to its original place then followed Edric and Mary away from the main asylum. Without regard for anything else, least of all being caught by asylum staff, Edric and I slipped into an abandoned building that sat on the outer edge of the asylum grounds. The fog still held its place in this location and served to conceal our movements the whole distance since we left the window behind. Once inside we found a rather convenient lantern sitting on a window seal inside the small building and lit it.

Luck seemed on our side at this moment and I began removing the sheet from Mary. I could see that she was still repeating her behavior loop, but then seemed to notice me. Her eyes widened as though she had not seen my face in a very long time. I worried that this meant that she was fading from our world, but I knew this to not be the case in my own heart. Immediately, Edric placed a cross in her hand along with some other symbol that seemed to be in the shape of an odd-looking hammer. I did not know what this symbol was, but it had a great effect on Mary as she began moaning and writhing in pain upon the leaves that had infested the dilapidated building.

My heart could not bear the suffering that Mary sustained at the moment, but I bit my emotions and choked them down. I could not allow this being to have any of my emotional self under its control. I could not be sure why I felt this way, but I knew this to be the case in every measure. Instead, I opened the Bible and began reading chapters and verses. I was not sure what might work, but it all seemed to have some effect. Mary's skin then began to make a sizzling sound as she cornered herself and tried to escape from our attempts to cleanse her. Then the moaning and growling began and her eyes began changing to a pale blue as they seemed to withdraw deeper into her skull. Her skin began to shrink upon her bones until she looked emaciated and weak but still maintained her strength tenfold.

I could only imagine the pain that she would be feeling at that moment, but I had to force my mind to deal with the task at hand. I continued reading from the Bible as Edric cut open one of his charges and began praying over Mary while putting an ashen cross over her forehead. To my surprise, she seemed to be gravely injured by this and immediately went limp upon the ground. It was then that the horrors started over anew and I could not hold my mind together with such a sight. Mary's flesh began bubbling under the surface as protrusions grew into tentacles fit for a giant squid of legend.

Each seemed to be covered in alternating patterns of ooze and rotting flesh that was controlled independently of each other as if new limbs were being formed. The tendrils emerging from her right side struck Edric which produced a horrible wail from both him and Mary as Edric was thrown through the window behind him. This prompted me to immediately throw a charge in Mary's direction and then shoot it to light the burner cap that I had placed inside at Edric's insistence. It was then that a wailing moan could be heard through the smoke in the room. This horrid setting then fell silent as the smoke cleared to reveal that Mary had escaped the room into the small wood outside the building.

It was not known to me how she had escaped without a greater presentation of sounds, nor if she remained in waiting outside the cabin for me so I moved to assist Edric in any way. I simply bolted through the doorway and looked toward the window which was now two yards from my present location. The thin glass had ruptured all over the ground as Edric was careful to take to his feet without harming himself further. He had begun muttering something about the smoke produced by the charges being harmful to someone possessed then produced one from his coat pocket along with a match.

In some cases, one would say that it was humorous to witness Edric moving about with the match and charge held out as though threatening someone with an unlit bomb. Yet this was no matter that would be regarded as humorous as the air itself hummed with fear and despair. I could feel as though I were being hunted by a much larger being which gave me the fear of being swallowed and devoured by such a being. There seemed to be a rustling sound coming from the trees on the other side of the cabin, but we couldn't verify the presence of anything.

Edric then lit the match and started the burn of the charge as he tossed the device onto the roof of the building. I had initially gasped with the worry that the charge would set the dilapidated structure and surrounding forest alight, but this worry quickly subsided as a guttural screeching emerged from the roof. I looked upward after drawing my pistol only to see something dart over my head and the sound of something heavy landing behind me. I turned with more swiftness than any human could possess and fired a shot directly into Mary's chest. I knew that the loaded shot was that of salt and gunpowder which performed its intended role as smoke began billowing from under the skin.

It was then that Edric launched himself forward and sliced one of the tendrils in two only to see black filth emerge and then dissolve upon the ground. The flesh of the tendril began burning where it had been cut as the blade had been silver-plated iron. Mary screamed unnaturally then darted forward and threw us both back and through the wall of the cabin. It was all that Edric and myself could do at this point to not be crushed by the wooden timbers that fell upon us. Yet we managed to do so without much difficulty or effort while digging ourselves free. Edric yelled as he was pulled from under the timbers and then wrenched toward a tree with great enough force to go silent instantly. As this happened his pistol fell to the ground while I rushed forward and took possession of it. I then slid before Mary and leveled shot after shot into her body. One shot after another rang out as I continued to fire and emptied everything I had into her.

She fell to the ground and writhed in pain with smoke rising which was then added to the charge that I lit and tossed upon her body. Immediately following this, I produced the Bible from under my coat and began praying once again only to finish by reading the word from passage after passage. I had never followed the selection with my eyes instead leaving it all up to chance and pushing myself to read whatever I had felt at the moment. The effect was to begin witnessing a smoky haze rising from Mary's person as I feared that she was beginning to die.

It was in this second that this haze took on a darkened form then began to separate from Mary completely. It was as I had hoped for her to be separated from this darkness and evil that infested her soul. I could see her struggling against it as well as her face was twisted with pain. It was then that a blast rang out and I was lifted from my feet for a moment only to be forced to the ground with such great pressure that I nearly fell unconscious. Everything had begun to become hazy in my vision and I moved my head from side to side while blinking to try to restore my vision. The only object I could see was Edric rushing to lift me from the floor of the wood as a ringing began in my ear and continued for a moment.

It was then that all sounds began rushing back to me until I heard a faint voice of Mary calling out for me.

"Benjamin?! Where am I, my love?" She asked.

I immediately rushed to her side and helped her from the ground with all the relief that I could hold in my heart. She recognized me right away as I pulled my coat from my body and placed it upon hers to cover her partially nude form. Edric had averted his eyes to respect Mary in her vulnerable state only to be addressed by our conversation.

"Who is this man Benjamin?"

I replied with as much information as I could give Mary at the moment without a proper setting for an in-depth conversation.

"This is Edric, my friend. He has helped me to save you from this beast and its terrible hold over your soul. I have suffered much without you my love and Edric has assisted to keep my focus on returning you to your usual loving self."

These words served to inform Mary that she was in good company as she thanked Edric and then wrapped her arms around me. I closed my eyes tight and fought back the tears and exhaustion that I felt from such an intense engagement with evil. I was simply overwhelmed by the idea that Mary had returned to me in such a complete and seemingly healthy state. It was then that I opened my eyes to see a darkened and heavy cloud reaching down toward the asylum until it had begun to cover the entirety of the island.

In an instant, all of my hopes and dreams were dashed and torn in two as Mary was jerked backward and pulled into the upper window of the asylum. I could only hear her screams and the breaking of the glass through which she had been pulled. At first, my mind could not comprehend what had happened, but this instantly changed to deep and writhing anger that seemed to have no end. I felt empowered and infuriated at the same time as a warmth overcame me while my mind and all senses focused. It was then that I turned to Edric to see him shucking more rounds into his pistol and approaching me. I followed by doing the same until I had refilled my gun then spun the cylinder only to click it back into the body of the gun.

Edric and I only had two charges for each of us left by my count, but I cared nothing about this at the moment. I did not wish to know such things as my heart kept my mind on this revenge and the fact that I felt I had enough rounds to wage war on the world itself. We approached the asylum and entered the building through the window from which we had originally escaped. However you would refer to this condition, as righteous fury, hate, or rage, I was no longer losing any focus at all. I entered the hallway and began moving quickly to the end, peering around the corner to see nothing but darkness which seemed hard to grasp. This was an unusual darkness that held some light adding a greenish hue to the world around me, but it did allow our eyes to see in most cases.

I approached the desk slowly and could see no one around the area, but I instinctively knew that I was being watched. It was then that I could see motion just on the edge of my vision to the right as a form darted to the top of the steps. I turned and began looking about the lower floor of the building as I did not wish to be ambushed at any time. I still had no idea of where anyone else would be contained as I was sure that the entire building had been full of people before this attack had begun. My mind did not race at this thought nor did I care but was instead maintaining my focus on the situation as I moved to the bottom of the stairs and began ascending them to the top.

I stood on the top landing of the stairs and waited to hear any unusual noises until the sounds of footsteps could be heard. It was at that moment that I could see a body step out of the far room in front of me and begin rushing my position. Instinctively I crouched slightly and placed my hand over the pistol with my ring finger hooked over the lever then fired a round into the man. I then quickly pulled the hammer again and locked it in place then waited. No sounds could be heard in the aftermath of the blast. This was a good sign, but still, a troubling one as Edric and I moved to the next floor above. We reached the landing as all hell broke loose and bodies came from all directions. We began firing one shot after another until each person lay unconscious on the floor.

Relentlessly, the sounds of more feet pattering across the flooring could be heard. I tossed a charge through the doorway and fired the only real round that I had loaded into it to set off the fire cap. This sent smoke and sparks in all directions as Edric and I took cover on the landing of the steps only to hear the moaning and screaming of each being followed by the thuds of bodies dropping to the floor. We both then knelt and quickly used our powder gauges to load each pistol then dropped the salt shot into each chamber and slid our lever to pack everything into place.

No footsteps could be heard, but the time it took to load our pistols gave a nerve-racking tension to the moment that was hard to describe. Fear and anxiety coursed through our veins as though they had replaced all blood pumped through us. Yet focus had won out in the situation as we knew that loading the guns correctly was the only way to deal with the situation without losing a hand in the fight. This was the last loading that could happen at this moment as only so much powder and rounds could be carried on our persons. We then took stock of our charges as we had maintained three for the upcoming fight. It was unfortunate, but we would have to utilize a more lethal method of defending ourselves. I produced a silver-plated bar whilst Edric held firm to a rod of iron that he had arrested from his home in haste.

I should state that it was not our most treasured option as we had no intention of knowingly killing anyone, but it had to be done in this more disastrous moment of self-defense. I would also wish to state that we had sorely underestimated our odds at this moment as we were sure that there would be no more defenses standing in our way. Yet we were wrong by any and every measure after proceeding into the hallway. We were only on the third of a six-floor building and already running low on rounds and powder. It was not the most sane or sound option to deal with in such a situation. This was only compounded by the fact that any defense had to be mounted in the dim black of the interior of the asylum.

Edric decided to take the lead as we moved into the common area of the third floor until we were backed into a corner once more. This time, however, it was all that we could do to not tire ourselves whilst swinging and parrying attacks from these crazed individuals. This darkness held a firm grip over these people until they were met with prayers and sacred metals. The only option at this moment was to crumple to the ground quickly and then begin writhing and moaning until being rendered unconscious. I had not noticed before, but smoke had begun to coalesce in the area while only rendering our visibility slightly strained.

The second revelation that I had in the aftermath of such chaos was that Edric now had a hold of his flask, but was using the device to disperse holy water unto the stained flesh of those possessed. It was then that we regrouped yet again to begin scouting the area for any others that might rush our location and attack without warning. We wandered through darkened corridors again and again as they seemed to twist further and in different directions. The most interesting was a corridor that was aligned in a diagonal direction to the rest of the building and left only one door to be searched now.

This hall seemed to be the darkest by far as no windows had been placed here nor did there seem to be any traditional rooms for patients in the area. The floors began creaking and buckling slightly underfoot as the whole of the area seemed to twist and distort the further that we moved. I could see the walls beginning to crack as they buckled inward suddenly while leaving a feeling of no footing followed by a falling sensation. Without warning, we were swallowed by a darkness that neither Edric nor I could understand. Just in the last moment, however, Edric was hanging in the dim light above me as he had caught himself on the floor above whilst I collapsed onto hardened ground below.

The falling sensation had ended only to leave me in pitch black and alone. The room into which I had fallen was cold in addition to the darkness that seemed to swallow everything. I did not know this place nor did I wish to, but I could not find a way out. I looked up to see Edric pull himself onto the floor above and then disappear for a moment until he poked his head out once more.

"Benjamin! Are you all right in there?!" He called out.

"I am fine, but how could this have happened? Were the floors not stable in this area moments earlier?" I asked.

Edric never answered these questions and instead tossed a lantern to me. It did not take me long to fumble for a match and light the lantern in the hopes that there would be enough oil to light my way. At that moment, I could see the shape of something in the dark all around me until I lit the lantern properly and turned the cloth to show more light. The horror sank into my chest of what I had come to know and witness as rotting and decaying bodies surrounded me. My mind could not come to terms with this sight which left my heart to process the understanding of what I was seeing. I did so hope that it was all an illusion, but the sight was real beyond measure. Yet no stench of decay hit my nostrils and the only thing left to be seen is what horrors would present themselves now.

This was all followed by the whooshing sound of something falling beside me and smacking onto the ground with a thumping sound that caused my heart to drop within my chest. I jumped to one side and drew my pistol until I realized that this was simply a rope.

"Get out of there, Benjamin! God only knows what horrors can come of this!" Edric exclaimed.

I left no time to waste and leaped onto the rope as Edric pulled with all of his might. I looked above me to see the flooring begin growing together as a tree growing in rapid timing. This was shocking enough, but to then notice that the bodies below were now writhing and moving toward the rope. Reaching up with their ruined and rotting flesh as their teeth gnashed and bit toward the open air.

I could hear a thousand voices whispering in the dark, calling me back toward them and to give in to the death that was desired. All of this is to only be followed by the feeling of soft, cold, and clammy hands grasping at my pants, ankles, and boots. It was the most uncomfortable feeling in my mind as I began climbing to get away from these bloated corpses. They continued piling on top of one another to reach me and grasp my feet to pull me under until I slid up and through the opening. The floor could then be heard popping as it closed together between Edric and myself. I could then feel a peace come over me until the sounds of banging and scratching could be heard. This was followed by the sensation that those souls below us were clawing and pulling at the flooring to escape.

My heart fluttered again as I clambered to my feet then grabbed tightly onto Edric's collar and coat; dragging him to his feet. We immediately made for the front of the building and the steps once more as hands and arms began bursting through the flooring in a grasping motion. The rot followed us along with a stench too great to describe to you as the hands continued to break through. Eventually, we reached the stairs with the lantern and turned to see nothing out of the ordinary. It was as I had hoped, an illusion crafted by evil to render one helpless to the darkness. We both took the time to gather our thoughts and breath until we noticed that our melee weapons had vanished. I knew that we had lost them in the fall from the third floor, but part of me hoped we would find them there above us.

8

The wood that supported the asylum itself creaked and made sounds of buckling as we moved back to the top of the stairs and rounded the corner toward the other set of steps. The darkness hugged the world around us tighter now and threatened to choke the beauty from all that we looked upon. The further we moved toward the top of the other stairs on the second landing, the darker and more melancholy the asylum appeared. It was as though we had been taken to another world entirely which gave Edric and I pause before proceeding.

It was then in that choking blackness that I placed my foot upon the top step and then heard the sounds of running, naked feet some distance away from me. I turned to Edric only to see him perk up immediately as if he had witnessed an apparition.

"Delilah? Is that you?" Edric stated as if lost in thought.

His words were more of a muttering that no one should have heard if not for us maintaining close support. Edric then began marching off into the darkness with purpose in each step. I could not see anything else around us in this darkness, but I was ready for anything even if it meant utilizing the small number of rounds that I had left.

I rounded the corner only to see Edric dashing into a darkened room that once held a patient. He called out into the void once more, but I could not make out what he had stated. I immediately pulled my pistol and held it firmly in both hands as I approached the room and began moving inside. It was then that I discovered only empty darkness and nothing more in addition to the silence that now filled the area. I had been deafened by the utter void that seemed to swallow all sounds as rapidly as they could be made. Even my foot-steps seemed to be fading faster than my ears could hear them.

That is to say that everything was audible but immediately forgotten as if I could no longer remember that each sound was made before. Something had begun taking hold of my mind and I knew it was nothing good. I tried with all my might to focus on the sounds of my breath while trying to recall the sounds of my footsteps. The whole of the room began to echo sounds from some unknown loca-tion as I moved further from the door. I looked all around me but it was simply an empty room with not so much as a scratch on the wood flooring. Surely a bed or some furniture would have been placed within this space to support any such life.

Eventually, I dropped my arms to my side in confusion and antici-pation for anything that could come next, but I had never prepared myself. A loud screeching could be heard from all directions that seemed to reverberate from the walls, through my body, and back to the structure around me again. Like a thousand bats infesting the walls and screaming in pain at the same time until I collapsed to my knees. It was as if the whole room had begun spinning with myself being the center anchor point. Then I saw them; dark and devouring the light from the lantern beside me.

All manner of forms had been stuck upon the walls, just standing in silence as if casting from a body in front of them. I could no longer focus long enough to count them or understand their shapes in detail. The only peace that I could find was that the screeching had stopped for the moment and I was glad for it. Yet I would come to find that my gun had been removed from my person and placed near the door. This was still some two yards to my left which seemed like an impassible chasm to cross. I knew that I was being taunted and guided to move toward the gun rather than think of my safety. I was a toy for these beings and their darkened plans and I would not stand for it any longer. I yelled out to God for safety as I leaned to my left and pushed up from the ground with all my might. It was enough to barely reach the handle of my gun as a rumbling could be heard all around.

The breath of my prayer still on my lips, I opened the side of the lamp and threw a pinch of one of the charges into it. This, I held out as I prayed and moved about the room. Smoke began moving with me until each of these shadow beings had been removed from their location. I began laughing slightly as I was filled with the confidence to fight such spirits. Then the light of the lantern was extinguished which cast darkness across every wall. It was an inky blackness that swallowed any light in the room. I rushed to relight the lantern again as I struck match after match in rapid motions. The moment seemed to stretch into eternity until one match finally lit the lantern just enough for me to look up and see Edric's face close to mine.

I jumped back in terror and drew my pistol toward his face only to see such a twisted and terrible anguished look. I could not know what he had just witnessed, but I could guess given my troubles. Edric then grasped the barrel of my gun and pushed it down toward the ground with a twisted and insane face being made all the while. My mind could only guess what he would do or say next, but I had the urge to move away from him. He pulled me to my feet by my ascot and then peered into my eyes as if gazing into my thoughts.

"She is not well, Benjamin! Delilah likes to play alone in the dark."

With these words, a larger smile seemed to stretch across his face from ear to ear as Edric's eyes rolled back into his head.

"I am the devourer, sir. It calls me to life to eat your wife."

Such a statement was now being uttered at a low volume from a voice that sounded like a young woman rather than the gruff voice that Edric would normally possess. Over and over these words began rising in tempo and volume until everything fell silent once more.

I shined the light of the lantern where he once stood, but I could see nothing. Surely Edric could not have dematerialized and left no trace of his physical existence. I could not explain what had happened to my colleague and friend. Yet he was nowhere in the room nor outside in the hallway leading up to the door either. Everything in me screamed to leave this place and find Edric later, but I could do no such thing. I could not leave him behind to whatever horrors held tight to his soul within this accursed place.

Instead, I stood firm and looked about the walls for any hidden doors or traps that could have formed from this evil. Still, I found nothing as evidence for such, but I kept looking on and on until I stood outside the door to the room. Now only darkness and still silence remained to greet me whilst a crushing feeling of isolation crept into my mind. Slowly I moved further and further from the door until I could see Edric standing at the bottom of the stairs and looking upward to the landing of the third floor. He was rigid in his stance and had lost his coat showing only his brown vest and white shirt that ran to his wrists.

The fabric of his shirt was pulled taught against his arms and had wrinkled in such a way to show the outline of his arms. Edric had been made into a statue of flesh and mortality, an example of the worst psychosis that I had witnessed. He whispered in the darkness with light filtering down to only show the slightest of details about him. I could feel a darkness that seemed to swirl around the location in which he stood, but I dared not approach. Still, the whispering grew louder and louder until I could barely make it out.

"Delilah, I cannot be free. He would not allow this for me. I am to wait for the man and devour his wife before him. Defile her beauty and womanhood before him to break his spirit. Pain, suffering...my love. Pain and suffering..."

Edric stated all of this whilst having his neck craned upward, extending so far that I could see his vocal cords moving with each gruff sound of the words spoken. How he could speak this way was beyond my understanding, but I knew that he was taken by something hollow and dark. Never would Edric speak of harming Mary in any way no matter the situation as he was not that dishonorable of a man. My heart had to come to grips with this understanding to keep silent within this dark place. I moved slowly and stealthily toward him with the lantern to my left side and hidden behind me partially. My right hand was preoccupied with my revolver and if needed, a charge from under my coat pocket cover.

I continued to approach until he turned to peer at me while keeping his neck extended in the same way. The appearance and mannerisms were all together unsettling, to say the least. Yet I held firm and moved steadily toward him with a reduced gate until he bolted up the stairs cackling all the way. This gave me pause for a moment until I realized that he was making his move toward Mary. I rushed the stairs with all haste that my legs could muster until I reached the third floor for the second time. I then held the lantern out in front of me and moved slowly, my gun held firm in my right hand.

"Delilah!" I called out. "Should it not be that you are lost? Driven mad by darkness? Your desires are not to harm Edric, I know this but you must also never harm her!"

I received no response from all of my efforts to be heard even while pausing to listen for shuffling feet as before. I wondered in the consuming darkness until I found myself lost in a portion of the third floor that was unfamiliar. I was alone and cold in this place, with little to show for my efforts to protect Mary. I hoped that Edric and Delilah had merged into one being and hidden away in this section. Otherwise, I would be wasting precious time that I could be reaching my wife. Though to do this would be to abandon Edric to whatever fate the darkness would relegate.

No, I felt Edric's presence now in this place. He was toying with me and my mental state and I knew that this would only go one way. I had to hunt Edric and bring him back into the light once more and if I found myself defending Mary then my friend must die. I moved to the end of the short hallway which held a bathroom on the right side and a window on the left in the middle. Light filtered gently in from the outside toward the middle of the hall but just barely lit one door at the other end. I moved to this door and peeked in with my gun at the ready, but I could only see the frame of steps greeting me in the darkness.

I held the lantern out to see them clearly and check for Edric in this place, but he was nowhere. I moved up the steps quickly and came into a very large and empty room with a single stream of light. I could see Edric sitting there as if on a chair but there was no furniture. His pose was that of *The Thinker* as he had been positioned to peer out of the window. I moved no further than the floor just beside the hole for the steps and made no sound. I could hear whispering no longer nor could I see any odd movements. I used this opportunity to gently and slowly place the lantern on the ground. Then I produced my last charge from my pocket and prepared it to be lit. My heart weighed heavy with this decision, but it had to be done. I did not wish to harm Edric nor allow this situation to linger until I would have to shoot him with the few real lead shots that I had. Lastly, I lit a match and held it to the fuse on the charge until it lit and began to sizzle slowly downward.

Edric still made no movements as I threw the charge just under him only to hear nor see anything. The charge did not go off and I wondered if the fire cap inside it had failed or gotten wet. Nothing changed with Edric, however, as he continued to peer out the window in such a horrid pose. I had no choice now but to either fix the charge and try again or shoot him with the salt round that I had devised. I had one extra fire cap if I could reach the charge and put it on top, I could light it ablaze again.

Naturally, I covered my bases and approached with my pistol held on his form in the darkness. Slowly but surely, I moved across the floor as quietly as I could muster until I was just behind Edric. It was then that his form seemed to melt away from a solid state and to that of a liquid. Nothing could have prepared me for such a sight, but I held firm until I could get the charge and then place the fire cap inside. As I was doing just that, Edric had reformed near the stairs in a menacing pose. He seemed to be seething with anger or a deep, psychotic rage, which I could not tell. I held the charge for a moment after I had fixed the fire cap then proceeded to toss it toward him. I then held a match in my left hand and my pistol in my right hand, but still, I waited for Edric's move.

Moment after moment passed until I could hear a growling sound that was unnatural, to say the least.

"Do something you beast! I no longer have time to waste upon you." I yelled out.

The next sound that could be heard was of a woman's angry tone uttered by Edric.

"The whore is not worth saving. We will treat her properly and with much pleasure for her flesh. Then she is devoured just like all the world...raped and devoured is what you all deserve!"

I then rushed forward with a battle cry as I struck the match and dropped to my side on the ground. I slid some distance as the beast began leaping toward me only to have the charge lit directly under it whilst I was able to slide to safety. I could see that the charge had its effect as Edric writhed on the ground until the shadow of a petite woman emerged from his body and stood motionless beside him. I then charged it once more and kicked the charge toward this form only to see an explosion of smoke and flame. The fire burned out quickly which left a thick fog that began falling toward the ground only to reveal that this form had been dispelled.

"Benjamin? What has happened?" Before Edric could say anymore, the room folded down upon itself and then faded to reveal that Edric and I were at the nursing desk on the third floor.

"Illusions, my friend. We are all illusions stuck in an illusion." I mumbled loudly.

My mind then fell firm upon the understanding now that this being was nothing more than an illusion. It could neither have a form nor harm unless we can be brought within this illusion. Connections were then formed within my mind which allowed me to understand everything that I could not before. The void is a trap that must expand itself into our world through illusions. It is neither present nor tangible, but it is a state where everything is disturbing but not real. Yet I knew this to only be a partial truth within the confines of reality as we know it to be currently.

The moment had changed, however, as I helped Edric to his feet only to find that his coat being gone was not part of the illusion. He looked about with the lantern that we shared, but could not find any trace of it. So too were the charges gone to leave us with two guns and homemade rounds with myself holding some lead rounds and a slight amount of powder. This would only amount to one more shot at best, but it would have to do. We did not allow this revelation to stop us as we moved on to the fourth floor and then to the fifth floor.

Still, we could see no way to the next and last floor in any corridor of this level. Perhaps this was yet another illusion or this was a demarcation between some security floors for the upper levels that patients would not be able to access. Neither of us could be sure so we stuck together as we moved from room to room. We had to clear the hallways and spaces between as well to make sure that nothing was missed. It was then that Edric stopped and turned to me outside the very last room to search.

"This is the last room and we have found nothing. Could it be that the sixth floor is a false floor? Maybe an inner floor within the attic?" Edric asked.

"I cannot say, but wherever the truth lies, it will be within this last room. Prepare yourself." I replied.

I then brushed past Edric and entered the room only to find myself in another place. I could also no longer find Edric anywhere around me. I could not recognize anything about this place, but I knew that it was all a part of another illusion or so I thought. That was until Edric appeared to me out of the dark and then motioned for me to follow him forward. We moved to the left of the door and into a closet where a hidden staircase had been placed. It was hard to understand why someone would build such a room, but it had to have been to hide the location of another floor from any patients.

I followed Edric's movements as we crept up the stairs and into an attic area that was utterly empty in every sense of the word. The rafters in the roofing of the building were normal, but as we followed the small amount that we could see in the dim space, we were met with a floor that looked odd. It was as if the floor were covered in oil, but it would not move or flow across the wood flooring. The surface of the flooring looked like a mirror, but one that shifts and distorts everything that it reflects. Edric and I simply stood on the stairs with our faces peering through the railing in front of us without wishing to move forward any further. I looked toward Edric, but he gave no response other than to shrug his shoulders. I felt that it was my duty to determine what we would do next in such an odd situation. I slowly made my way to the landing to observe the floor closer but noticed that the floor was now less reflective. Now there seemed to be a depth to whatever this substance would be on the wood. I reached out and wiped the flooring, but there was nothing different than touching a wooden floor.

My mind had prepared me for something wet, cold, and oily but the feeling was nothing odd in the least. I then moved my hand further forward toward the middle of the substance only to realize that there was a pulling sensation. I resisted at first but felt compelled to allow myself to cooperate with the mental commands that I was being given. I knelt and then pushed against the flooring only to have it break away and swing into an alternate world. Edric was not far behind, but his arrival was interesting as well as it seemed like he was rotating into the world from the one that was left behind. My mind struggled to understand whether this world was the real world and the other was a false world that we had been forced into. *Had we simply slogged through a horrible swamp of isolation and fear?* Now Edric and I stood upon a stone ground that seemed suspended within a never-ending night.

Nothing could indicate whether the dark surrounding us stayed on the same level as the platform which we inhabited, but neither of us wished to test this. Instead, we both refocused ourselves and moved across the platform toward a door on the far side. The closer we came to the door itself, the more we could notice that the door was not placed within a wall. The darkened background remained in the distance as the door did not move. The sentiment within my mind was that I would attempt to open the door, but it was falling from its place. This, of course, was not the case as the door opened without issue to a lit space that seemed more like a hotel than anything else.

Candles flickered within their glass holders upon the wall which illuminated alternating black and red tapestries that lined the hallway on both sides. The flooring was darkened but not the same void that was within the previous space. Yet both seemed to have a void of no sound that accompanied the spaces. Now it seemed that our minds struggled to cope with the reality of this space as nothing of the like could exist. The catch to it all was how would this structure be supported over nothingness while also being illusionary, yet real.

Edric began moving forward slowly whilst I would follow just off his right side as we both searched for a doorway or opening to move out of this space. Nothing seemed to be clear, however, yet as we came closer to the far wall at the end of the hallway, I could hear something. It sounded as though a woman sobbed from behind the wall, but this sound seemed to reverberate throughout the hallway. My initial instinct was to say that this would be Mary, but I was not convinced as the voice sounded slightly distorted toward a deeper tone. It was as though something was mimicking her voice to add to the stress of the situation.

Edric said nothing until we reached the wall and then began feeling around for a space to move forward.

"What is this place? Edric stated.

The words were not clear, however, due to a sound distortion that seemed to hang in the air all around the space. I simply nodded my head and brought the butt of my pistol upon the wall to see it swing forward and fall into a barn-like scene with Mary nowhere to be found. The space was dark but real enough to give the sense that I had entered a barn.

The flooring of the barn seemed to have a darkened mist that flowed from below it to form a shape that was bulbous at its core with great arms and legs that jutted out of the central form. It was the oddest sight until shapes that seemed like eyes that flittered from red to yellow opened in the upper and center portion of the central shape. The whole of the sighting was odd, to say the least, but still interesting rather than threatening. Still yet, the voice began emanating from the being but now twisted even further.

To our horror, however, an arm began emerging from the body of the being until the form of a woman who had been burned on one side emerged. She stuck out of the body from the waist up and seemed partially decayed. There were no indications as to how this was happening, but it was real enough. The bodies of other women would emerge from the upper portion as well, but being cut in many places rather than being burned. I felt that I knew these women, but I would not dare speculate in my time of focus. Now the sounds that emanated from the being changed to a moaning sound that denoted agony and pain. The voices were instantly recognizable, but not distracting in the least. My mind was resolute now and I had become more focused than ever to make this being suffer.

Before I could act in any way, Edric stepped forward and threw the last charge in front of this being as I pulled my pistol and fired. The charge burst into flames as the smoke obscured the being which left it screaming in a horrible tone that hurt my ears to even experience. Edric continued to move forward as I blasted another shot through the smoke and into the being once more. I had expected this thing to move from its current location, but it had been stunned by the charge. I no longer doubted the effectiveness of the charges against the pure demonic being at that moment. Edric and I now used the time given to hurt this being further in any way that we could with him slashing the being with his knife while I landed shot after shot.

The confrontation was short-lived, however, as this beast exploded and seemed to dispel its form completely to only fade to a smoking puddle. A faint moaning emanated from all around us in this realm whilst the ground seemed much less solid with every passing moment. It was then that we were expelled from this world to fall from the rafters of the first floor of the asylum and collided with the ground. The force itself knocked the air from Edric and my lungs completely which left us writhing upon the floor of Mary's room. I could then feel hands resting upon my chest as I heard Mary's lovely voice calling my name.

Such a sweet sound pulled my mind together slowly until I realized that I was resting on the wooden floor with Mary gazing upon me from above. I could see that the hold that this being had over her was gone which gave my heart the rest that I had longed for since the previous evening. I sat up and peered over to Edric who was now climbing to his feet as he brushed his shirt with his hand. Before I could rise to my feet, Edric had already moved past Mary and me to the door to listen for anyone approaching.

Neither of us had a plan to remove Mary from this place, but it seemed that Edric had formulated one already. Mary helped me to my feet as I brushed myself off and then clung to me until she witnessed my ability to walk.

"Someone is coming this way. We have to leave now!" Edric whispered.

I said nothing but gave a nod in acknowledgment then we proceeded from the room and down the hallway. We used the same window that we had left the asylum through and then removed ourselves from the asylum grounds completely. Edric, Mary, and I moved swiftly and quietly back to the dock which was still shrouded in fog. We had hoped that this fog bank would conceal our location if the guards of the asylum would take notice of Mary's escape.

We approached the dock and called out for the captain of the ferry only to hear the engine start and the boat begin pulling from the dock. Edric rushed ahead of us with Mary just behind him and myself bringing up the rear. Edric leaped upon the boat as I caught up to Mary and helped her across which left just enough time for me to jump over to the deck of the ferry. I had been lucky enough to land one foot upon the deck balancing myself and not fall back into the water below. We all then made our way to a bench that was set just outside the main cabin of the vessel and waited to arrive at the other dock.

Unlike the journey to the island, the return trip seemed to go much quicker and without event. The waters were no longer as choppy under the boat whilst the fog bank that covered the area had lifted completely. My mind raced with the worry that our captain would question why we had left for the island with two and returned with three people, but this did not occur. Instead, we reached the other dock only to have him bid us a farewell and a good day. We crossed the dock swiftly but without rushing then entered a coach that had arrived conveniently. Once the door had been shut, we all breathed a sigh of relief the refocused ourselves on the long journey to Edric's home. The streets of the city seemed less gloomy and filled with a comforting and radiant light throughout the ride. I could feel that we were free from the burdens of this haunting whilst realizing that I had been eager to reach Mary and my home to relax without tension in the air. The remainder of the coach ride was in silence and I could see that we were all too fearful to speak of the events of the past few days.

I knew that Mary and myself were the most relieved as it seemed that we had been relieved of insurmountable stress in our family life. We had been without peace within our home for some time now as it seemed that I had become accustomed to suffering with oppression and fear. My mind had also begun to race with the possibilities for Mary and myself and relax in a life of comfort and luxury since my acquisition of the bank. Since my childhood, I had longed for a life of luxury and ease to enjoy the world and have the time to see the world's beauty.

A few streets later, we arrived in front of Edric's home as we bade him a good day and watched him leave the coach and move into his home. I could see the roses that grew across trellising on the right side of the home which marked a pass beside his home and to the next street. The roses were an interesting contrast with the white of

Edric's home and the same color being displayed from the picket fence beside this pass. It was then that my eye focused upon the same man from the train standing under the roses and peering back at the coach. I knew that I had witnessed this man watching the coach, but my mind could not process that he would be in such a familiar location.

9

The next morning held only light shining through our bedroom window while also marking the first night without horrid and dark dreams. The rest that Mary and I received was much needed and not without praise from my mind and body together. Mary still rested as I removed myself from the bed and began dressing yet I could not help but worry that she might not wake. It was an irrational fear, but I felt it necessary given all that had happened to her in the previous days. I checked Mary's health with the mirror under her nose which gave me peace of mind that she was alive and well.

I knew in my heart that she would be able to rest now without the worry that something would take her in her dreams. My heart felt peace and understanding that this could all be over now leaving only our lives to live. Such a realization gave me the satisfaction to know that we could overcome evil forces that threaten our lives. While I still did not understand everything to its minute details, I was able to be comfortable with some methods of defense. Our home was now a sanctuary once more from the world that raced around us. An escape that was much needed now that I had invested so much into the bank and its success.

I made my way down the stairs and into the sitting room of our home only to bring my pipe to bear and begin puffing away on the morning's peace. The birds were chirping outside along with a midsummer's dew upon the leaves. Flowers bloomed along the windows in the front of our home with all manner of people wandering the streets. Every puff of tobacco brought more images that flashed in my mind of the hardships that I had faced until now. All of this would culminate in the success that I could now feel, but also inspire the moves that I would make in the coming days.

My focus was to bring all of my talents to bear in running the bank from afar and allowing another person to rise to the position that I had once held. This was the way of enterprise in our great country along with the dreams being fulfilled by others moving forward within their career. I was happy to move out of the way of another person's future successes within the bank. Perhaps it would even progress to my selling of the bank to that same person to further my rewards in life. I continued pulling from my pipe and rolling my tongue around the mouthpiece as I thought on these subjects.

I could hear Mary making her way down the stairs and toward the smoke that billowed from the sitting room. I knew that her rest would allow her to ask to leave the home and enjoy the sunny day, but I also felt that I would have to attend to business first. Mary rounded the corner to stand in front of me with such a lovely and bright disposition on her face.

I could feel that my beautiful wife was now present again and not being attacked by something otherworldly. This gave me comfort and happiness to know that level of freedom in our lives.

"My love. Shall we go out of the home today? I would enjoy the park on such a beautiful and warm day." She stated with a peaceful tone.

"I would love to do so, but I also must attend to the bank today. Could we accomplish breakfast with my business then we shall rest in the park?"

"That would be possible, yes, my love."

With her agreement on our plans for the day, I placed my pipe into my mouth and walked to the door, opening it for Mary. I never bothered to remove my pipe or stop smoking it after leaving our home but simply strode along with Mary toward our breakfast destination.

The streets were not overly crowded but held many people who also rushed along to one destination or another. Some had come to our neighborhood for relaxation while others had arrived here for business with other companies. Mary held a wonder in her heart once more as she looked about the street and took in the sights as if seeing them for the first time. I was glad that she was back to enjoying the world with youthful enthusiasm as she had done just a short couple of weeks before.

The walk was brisk in the morning air even with everyone else occupying the streets which ended with our walking into a restaurant as before. I was no longer bashful in bringing my wife into the eatery and simply asked the waiter to seat myself and present company. I felt that it was a shame to have to declare such things in our modern world, but it was the culture of our times. Yet no one seemed to react in any way to Mary and I eating together and simply seated us properly and with care. We then proceeded to order the same food that we had on our first visit to this restaurant and then sat across from each other talking.

I had finished my pipe and placed it into my pocket whilst within the restaurant but still felt the urge to relax in such a way. Though now I had become involved in my conversation with Mary as I explained the details of what had happened to her. She was appalled by the thought that something had begun controlling her mind and body while also expressing disdain for anyone who would bring about police involvement. We both knew that someone would have to have been on the street hearing the sounds from two nights before then running to the officer on the corner of our neighborhood to bring their attention to all that was going on.

I had never expected such a reaction, but the need to keep the peace in the city was overwhelming in its reach. Still, I was fortunate for the sudden setting of our supernatural battle on the asylum grounds. Witherbrook still loomed in my mind, however. No matter how many topics that Mary and I could work through in a conversation. The whole island intrigues me given the feelings when in those surroundings. I could not be certain if this was the norm of weather that far into the bay, but the fog added certain protection.

Though my mind tells me that this would be only a coincidence, I know that the truth is it was all more than a coincidence. The forces that influenced our mission to save Mary seemed to protect themselves from being known to others as well. Such beings seem to gain power and confidence within the shadows, but bringing them to the light would not be enough. The fundamental understanding of this "void" seemed to be an aversion to being known and predicted. Mary continued with her point within our conversation as my mind processed the events of the previous day. I could not understand the place that Edric and myself have taken upon entering Witherbrook the second time. The whole interior of the asylum was cold and dark, but not unreasonably dark. It seemed to be designed to cause pressure on anyone who could never focus in such a situation.

Such things were then pushed to the back of my mind as our food and drinks arrived at the table. The usual formalities followed then the waiter left once more to attend to other customers. Mary began eating immediately as she seemed famished beyond all capability of a woman of her stature. I was sure that this was simply a side effect of being possessed, but I could not be sure. Eventually, however, my thoughts were broken by Mary asking:

"What is the business that you will need to see to, my love?"

I could feel the eager excitement as she said those words, but I had a reluctance to boring her with the details of my plans for the bank. Instead, I replied, "We will travel to the bank this morning and attend to lifting another person into the position that I had held. My employees will need to know about the sale of the bank and it would be a privilege to hear anything that they would have to say."

Mary simply nodded in response and never gave any indication that she would oppose our visiting the bank.

We continued in this way until the end of breakfast and the passing of money to the counter at the front door. I was more than eager to go about my day and not remain in the restaurant so I handed the tip over to the waiter in person and apologized for my rudeness, but he did not seem offended. Instead, he gladly grasped the money from my hand and nodded to me in thanks as I moved to the street outside. Mary followed closely as we turned toward the bank and began walking to the other end of our street.

We hailed a coach and rode our way through the streets until we had reached the beginning of downtown and continued down the street until we reached the bank. I stepped out of the coach first then helped Mary behind me down to the street. Straightening ourselves, we proceeded to the doorway of the building. The door was graciously opened by the attendant to a hearty thanks by myself and Mary. I then called out for the tellers and others to approach and hear what I had to say.

Everyone gathered around as I had begun to address each employee.

"I am glad to be here with you all again, but it is in a different capacity now. I have returned from North Carolina with a new wife and a decision that had to be made. I am pleased to announce that I am purchasing The Northeast Bank and am now responsible for any decisions that must be made. I will no longer manage the bank and am currently looking for another to take my place. Please talk with me as such in my office currently. Thank you all for your hard work and dedication. Have a productive work day!"

I then moved to the lower offices and met with the finance office. There I vigorously signed the paperwork to officially purchase the bank. Tension lingered in the air as I shook the hand of Mr. Sorghum's representative.

"Thank you, sir! I have awaited this moment for several years. Please relay to Mr. Sorghum that I am pleased with his decision to accept my offer and thank him for me." I stated.

I placed several coins into the man's hand as he finished rolling the documents into a cylinder and sliding them into a protective case.

Mary and I then made our way up the oak staircase and rounded the banister to the left only to enter my old office. Mary immediately began looking about the room in amazement that this was my office where I spent most of my time. It was not long before a gentleman entered my office and asked to speak with me about the management position. He was a delightful fellow who did seem to have a business mind, but I was not able to understand what he would be able to accomplish as a manager of the bank. I knew that what he said was correct in every way, but he had no confidence in the position. This was not a requirement, however, so I informed the man that I would be there for two hours that morning and to remind anyone who might be interested.

He nodded eagerly with a smile then turned and rushed out the door and down the stairs to the teller floor. I followed to the banister and watched the man return to the teller desk and wait for another customer to help. He was nothing more than a regular teller, but I would not discount this given my history within the bank. I knew that anyone could manage the bank and surely someone so humble might take the business in a better direction. I simply wished to know that the man would not be intimidated by anyone seeking to invest in the bank. Though he was a nice man of the age of about thirty but seemed slightly older.

I would consider him, however, as he was the only one who came forward with interest in the position. I then sprang into movement and pulled the records from the main office that served the owner well. I pulled the personnel file for the man and immediately began studying each page. It was not a normal practice to build a file for an employee but Mr. Sorghum felt it necessary to know who each person was and what they brought to the bank. Now I would use the same files that I thought an oddity to decide what would need to happen with a new manager. I felt only right if I were to give anyone a chance in the same way that I was given such a chance. I placed the man's file on my desk and perused the few pages that it contained. Upon reading the page of his qualifying background, I discovered that he was a man capable of managing larger banks than this.

Mr. Eaber had been recommended by some rather large banks within Boston and seemed to have managed a larger bank more recently. The file did not indicate why he had begun working here as a simple teller, but I felt that he would be the better man for the job. Though I was sure that others would not accept the job due to my purchase from the bank. I felt no resentment in this as I had only proven myself to be capable as a manager in the eyes of those under me. I found myself wrapped within my work for much of the time in managing the bank and never able to attend to my employees. I hoped that I would be able to make up for that now and would never have to remove myself from the bank completely.

It would now mark the time that I would be able to invest in the bank itself and fix the items that would damage a building's reputation. The only option now would be to speak with a friend of mine with the chosen construction company. Mary and I remained in the office for the rest of the allotted two hours without another visit.

We left the office and locked everything behind us without any further conversations. Mary and I moved to the lower level and to the teller desk which I then entered and turned the keys to my office over to Mr. Eaber. He was ecstatic to be chosen for the management position. I explained to him that I would return in two days to make sure everything was going well, but that he would start his new position the next morning. I left the bank to its business and to operate without my hands being involved at every step as was in the past. Now Mary and I waved to everyone as we left the building and stepped out onto the streets.

It was then that I bumped into a younger man who stopped and apologized to me.

"Good sir, where is it that you are hurrying?" I asked the man.

"I am sorry sir, the fair is starting soon and I am trying to catch a taxi." He then nodded and waved his hat to Mary then boarded a passing taxi.

I looked toward Mary to only be met with an interested look in visiting this fair. The only next step was to board the next taxi and ride it to the destination at this new attraction. It seemed that many people would be joining us to see what wonders would await at such a gathering. We both took in the sights as we passed through portions of the city rarely viewed in my everyday life.

Eventually, we both had begun to notice a beautiful and underdeveloped area begin to emerge from the modern sprawls of the city. The trees were greener and the air slightly cleaner here than near our home. Immediately the shock of seeing a vibrant and colorful glass and an iron building emerged from the landscape as if being raised before us. People had flocked to this area as I had never witnessed in my life though I could understand the urgency given such a beautiful and intricately built structure. Though what would be contained within such a structure would be the true interest of anyone attending the fair.

Upon entering the building, I was struck dumb by the sight of colorful flags being hanged from each section of iron. The glass was wonderfully tinted in such a way as to allow light, but reduce the heat coming into the building. It was a truly magnificent work of art from beginning to end. Two levels of attractions along with shops are being set up in some areas. People also sold merchandise and some food along the way to the location of the fair. In any case, this was a truly impressive undertaking that seemed to have improved upon the designs two years earlier in England.

Both Mary and I were drawn into the immaculate design of the architecture like moths to a flame. I could not take in all of the sights at once as each new detail engaged my senses in a wrap of intrigue in tantalizing beauty. I was sure that our mouths hung open while viewing the interior for the first time. The only reduction of such sights was that of an awkwardly placed statue in the center of the forum. It was that of George Washington upon a horse, but it was a horrible interpretation of what the real statue would look like. Almost as if the original had been broken so the sculptors introduced a cheap remake instead.

Other than this, we had been pleasantly surprised by the event itself. Nothing could compare to a summer's day that had come a fortnight into July. The only other intriguing sight was that of the people that wandered throughout the structure. Every color and nation seemed to be represented within this cultural center of American power and dominance. I could feel the vision for the future of our great nation reflected within this powerful image of national pride. Many today would contend that such a fair was America's attempt to entertain the level of nobility from other nations. I would see this more as showing that our nation can rival the likes of such nobility and innovate above the achievements of what they have accomplished.

This was the American way in every sense of the word while showing that we too could occupy the leading of the world with culture, architecture, and engineering. I could even spy a display from the Colt Gun Company in the distance along with opulent statues of fine art that put the main statue in the gallery to shame. Greek revival was now in full swing as had been predicted just a year earlier as well. Such calls to the ancient world were refreshing, to say the least as art seemed more elegant in its more original forms.

All of this was to be met by a band playing many patriotic themes from outside the venue with great accuracy. Each note seemed to flutter into the building as a flock of butterflies escaped those who walked through their tall grasses. Amazement was not a strong enough word for such an event as it was all to capture the heart of every nation from around the world while celebrating our great nation. The only thing that seemed to cheapen the experience was that of the side shows that begged for on-lookers to flock to his stalls. None of these ideals sat well with Mary or me, though Mary was interested in the doctors practicing bloodletting among other such practices.

Only one dollar for a day of gawking about within all of this artful beauty and opulence seemed to be appropriate. Though this admission would only cover walking about and nothing purchased within the building. Mary was immediately drawn to a compartment that displayed fine-cut jewelry along with other baubles. I stood about anticipating a question to purchase such jewelry from her, but she seemed to be less interested than I had once thought.

"Did you not wish for more jewelry, my love?" I asked.

"I am sorry, Benjamin. But I am not interested in having such gaudy jewelry rather than something less materialistic. I am not such a woman to want a thing such as this jewelry, though I will not refuse it from you, my love. I would rather not seek these items out of my own accord, however." She replied.

Mary now stood glowing with beauty from every portion of herself. She was such a powerful and amazing woman for resisting the temptations of wants from needs within our world. I could see that her practical sensibilities were what I craved within a match for my lifestyle. I seemed to be drawn to taking in her beauty more so now than before as she had struck me within my heart.

Then it was that we came upon another statue that stood shockingly prominent within the gallery. This was the beauty of The Naked Lady on display which seemed to reflect that of Mary's beauty. Some were averting their eyes when it came to such a sight, but others seemed to read a plaque that stood along with the artwork. Upon reading, it was explained that this woman was a Greek slave being sold in an auction that seemed to be more comfortable with onlookers. I was, of course, more removed from that notion and enticed by the idea of displaying the gentle and fiery curves of such a gentle creature as of a woman. I simply leaned to my left and whispered into Mary's ear, "This is the beauty of my wife represented within eternity."

I could see that Mary wished not to hear such things at first until my words had reached her inner thoughts. At which time she was enthralled by my words and seemed to take a flirty stance now rather than disgust. Thought it was our nation's first reaction to avoid nudity at all costs within our society, but I was not feeling such. I cared not for her nudity, but more for the form and style that it represents. I cared not that she was representing a slave, but rather that of a woman who stood bold and comfortable within herself. Such ideas were new to our societal structure, but I felt to embrace this change rather than avoid that which is inevitable.

Mary and I now moved to the Colt showcase as I began immersing myself in the rifles and sidearms that had been displayed.

I did not waste time picking out a newer version of my pistol. I provided an offer to the salesman to take my pistol for a reduced price, which was not refused. Instead, I paid the full price while keeping my original firearm for refashioning. My new Colt revolver was of such fine craftsmanship that I could not help to lay money upon the display. The man even loaded it for me and provided another container of powder to me.

The last stop that was made before leaving the fair was to stop and purchase perfume for Mary. She loved the lavender scent and floral scent of the perfume along with the feeling on her skin when she sampled the product. I had to agree as she smelled beautiful as a meadow filled with flowers. We then left the fair proper and moved back toward the other stalls in search of drinks and food. Mary walked gracefully beside me without tugging in any noticeable way upon the grasp that she held around my arm. Her dress flowed along with her giving the appearance that she would be floating across the ground.

Very little time had passed before we reached a stall that sold both food and drink. I partook of a whiskey as Mary tried something new. It was called R. White's Lemonade and seemed to please Mary's taste completely. We found a bench upon which we would rest and partake of our food. My initial instinct was to move further along the street to see more, but Mary was tired and we both could feel the heat of the day beating down upon us. I felt much better knowing that I had forgotten my jacket at the bank. The early morning seemed to indicate a storm or rain, but this had never happened.

We walked along the road between the stalls without refreshments in hand while enjoying the sun. A breeze had now begun to blow through the streets wicking away any amount of heat that had been felt upon our skin. This factor coupled with the food and drink, gave Mary and me a great sense of ease while being exposed to the elements. All around we watched people looking about the stalls while also carrying their own purchased items. Souvenirs were all the rage from the fair, but Mary and I did not wish for such clutter within our homes. Instead, we both enjoyed more of the smells and tastes of the food stalls while sharing these moments. It had truly become a special event even with multitudes of people flocking about the area.

Perhaps an hour had passed from the time that we arrived to check the stalls on the street and left the Crystal Palace behind. We knew that it was time to leave by taxi and return to our area of the city, but stopping at the park along the way. We piled into the taxi and finished the last bits of our food while Mary slowly savored the drink she had purchased. The journey to the park seemed to go much smoother than the ride to the fair had. The added benefit of the gentle breeze also aided in our enjoyment as well. We arrived at the park only to move under a tree in the area and take in the day. People moved throughout the park but did not seem to stop as they had on other days. It seemed that the fair had finally begun to attract more of a local group to its exhibits. Normally we would have taken the time to gently place a blanket amongst the uneven grounds around the trees in the park. Today we did not do much but walked around the grounds of the park to see the many bushes that had been styled. There were also water features that pulled us toward it for a refreshing spray of water.

It was in this lull that my mind had begun to wonder how Edric had fared since our last mission together. I would have expected his visit to our home to inform me of discoveries that had been made. My first thoughts were that of Edric immersing himself within his work or personal life for a taste of normalcy. He was a man who did not like to lose his vision for his research and work for the colleges of our city. His research had caused Edric to reach new heights within his professional career and amongst his peers. He had been called upon because he could understand and speak several languages. Thus he would travel to different countries and represent the research partners of our nation.

Immediately I took Mary's hand within mine and asked, "My love, would we visit Edric on this day? I wish to know if he has had troubles since the events of the asylum."

Mary said nothing at first but agreed after some thought.

"I would not mind this, but we do need to rest together after such events," Mary replied.

I agreed with her in every way but knew that any visit to Edric would not take too much time from our day. Edric was not accepting of frequent guests, but I felt it was my duty to check in on his health. Perhaps it was that I had tapped into an understanding put upon my mind by a higher power. This would indicate that it was needed for me to check in on Edric and his mental state. I would hope that he did not have an infestation of his own, but such was the way with this demon. Surely it would have known that Edric had involved himself and wished to attack him if it still lived. Though I was sure that no such thing had happened since Edric seemed much more capable and immersed in the supernatural than I.

Mary and I stood for a few moments more while embracing each other in love and affection. It was not the proper thing to do in our time, but I cared not for the desires of the decency of others. I had become a man more proud to be alive than caring for social norms and acceptance. Instead, I would hold Mary close any chance that I could and position my kisses to be the most romantically engaging. After all, I had sacrificed much for her love and fought all odds to bring her to New York with me. I would not allow myself to miss any moment of a woman who could have been lost for eternity to some foul creature. I cherished our love and time together now more than before.

Though after some time we did depart from the park and walked the city block to Edric's residence. Mary enjoyed this approach most as she was able to see the red roses growing in the alley beside his home. She was not approving of red roses in the least but loved to see their growth all the same. It was the white variety that Mary preferred and I was happy with such a division in what she desired. We then rounded the corner and approached Edric's door only to be met with a notice upon his door that he had departed the country for Europe that morning. I peered through the side window of his entryway and could confirm the darkness that was the interior.

I prayed to myself for Edric's safety as he shortly traveled to

Europe. It was not a passage that was the most dangerous but still was not safe by any measure. Ships had been lost at sea multiple times on the northern Atlantic and probably more still that had not been known. I knew that he would be safe, however, and instead pulled Mary for her to join me in walking along the street. We moved at a slower pace now while conversing about our activities for the rest of the evening. The sun was now beginning to hang itself lower in the sky and I felt no urge to consume any amount of food. I knew this eliminated the need to cook or eat within our home. Without these needs, Mary and I would be free to play a game or enjoy our porch and talk with whiskey within our hands.

"Thank you so much for providing my drink at the fair. It was delicious and sweeter than anything I have drank before." Mary stated.

I replied that I was more than happy to provide such a beverage to her and suggested that we should travel to our home on foot to enjoy the rest of the sunlight. Though we did not have very far to travel, I knew that the sights would slow us down as we took them in. As we traveled by foot toward our home, Mary and I could see that the fair had drained people from the streets. The shops that were normally open during typical hours had closed for the rest of the day.

This was a stark contrast with our normal sights within the city, but it was a refreshing sight in any case. Not having to fight through the congested streets at certain hours of the day was a very attractive prospect. This was not something that could happen for our city to maintain itself on any given day, but it was welcomed on some days. Now the sights of the city had become its wonderfully diverse architecture that was no longer inhibited by the people wandering about on the streets. Mary and I continued toward our home at a steady pace as the sun dimmed behind us. It was now that I could be comfortable relating to Mary given our shared experiences as such I promised her that I would explain more to her about these happenings. It was now my objective to ensure that Mary was told everything about my experiences within North Carolina. I was sure that she would lose all sanity after experiencing her possession.

10

Mary and I reached our stoop as the sun dipped below the horizon. I could only see the lock upon the door in the glow of orange and purples that accompanied the dying day. I quickly turned the lock to the right and then pushed open the door only to feel an intense reluctance to enter. I felt the urge to pull my new firearm in anticipation that I would be attacked. Instead, I was met with silence and stillness save for the house settling in the late evening air. I slowly moved into the entryway of the home and allowed Mary to move past me as I shut the door. The air still seemed off as though I was entering where I did not belong, but I could not see or hear anything out of the way. I simply shrugged it off and locked the door with a gentle turn of the lock. I followed Mary deeper into our home as she produced the bottle of whiskey and two cups. Immediately we moved to the back porch and took our seats only to pour two glasses full and talk.

The evening held humidity that was light and not oppressive, but still did not allow for much relief. Instead, we had opened the back windows of the home to allow for it to breathe. I worried that the heat would trap itself within the structure and stifle our attempts to sleep peacefully, though I did not have to anticipate anything other than such. Mary rocked in her chair with her head back and her eyes closed while only taking the occasional sip of her glass. I could not help but stare at her beauty as she sat motionless like the statue we had gazed upon within the fair.

I would have compared her beauty to any other woman claiming to be the most beautiful. Yet I was sure that I would be biased in this way and perhaps not see Mary in the same light as others. Though this did not factor into my views of Mary at any given moment. It was only important that Mary was made for me and would only be understood by myself. Eventually, this was broken by the loud clip-clopping of horses pulling coaches down the streets all around our home. The sun had set completely as Mary lit a lantern outside the home. The dim light gave a haunting glow to our home and each other in this thick darkness. Though I did not care, I could see that Mary had become slightly apprehensive now and somewhat uncomfortable. I tried to ignore this as I packed and lit my pipe having only the troubles associated with dim light.

"Has something bothered you, my love?" I asked Mary.

She said nothing at first and simply shook her head, but she held a look upon her face that seemed as though she had fallen ill. Her skin did not change to a sickly hue, but her expression indicated it all the same. I was sure that she had become uncomfortable with the air where we sat but did not wish to worry me.

"My love, if something is happening to you then I must know!"

Mary said nothing once more but still seemed to be holding back a sickness that had afflicted her suddenly. It was as though something had taken her peace now, but I could not be sure of the origin. Some time passed as Mary began to recover from her sudden sickness. She would sit for a moment more in silence but seemed to be collecting her thoughts.

"I am sorry my love, but I have suddenly been struck with nausea. Perhaps I have drank too much. I think I am going to bed if you don't mind." Mary stated.

Of course, I had not cared for her to leave for bed and I even helped her up the stairs, undressed her, and helped her to slip under the coverings of the bed. I then returned to the back seating area and continued to puff upon my pipe and finish my whiskey.

The time had reached nine o'clock before I had smoked every bit of tobacco within my pipe. I stood from my chair and moved back into the house armed with the lamp from outside. The oddities of our home were never more prevalent than now. The darkness seemed to be a living entity that was being forced back from me by the light. It seemed that the shadows shifted and swirled all around, but was not completely obscuring my vision. Instead, it seemed that I was able to make out faint shapes shifting within the darkness.

Some shapes seemed tall and some seemed short, but all were darker than the surrounding darkness. They did not seem to move about other than appearing to dance around the light from the lamp. I know that I would have been questioned after drinking a glass of whiskey, but I knew that this was nothing to me. I would have never been affected in such a profound way by just one glass of whiskey. I simply decided to forget these shapes as shadows cast in odd ways by the lamp.

I was, however, still affected by seeing these shapes as my heart had begun beating faster. My muscles tensed and I could feel my hand upon the handle of my pistol. I anticipated that I would be thrust again into a world of shadows and evil, but nothing happened in the moments that I checked the windows and doors on the lower level. Upon catching my hand in the action of escalating my situation, I removed my grip on the handle of my pistol and moved up the stairs as smoothly as I could. I hoped that these beings would not understand that I had witnessed their shape or presence within my home. I moved as quickly, but as gracefully as possible, but the further that I moved, the more apparent it became that they were real. I topped the stairs and happened to catch movement from the edge of my vision. I turned toward the guest bedroom but could see nothing until I held out my lantern. It was now that I could see the image of a little girl crouched in the corner, but she was made of shadow.

It seemed as though these beings were real in every way, but were out of place in their dress and actions. I could not understand why this was but I could not stop myself from continuing to bed. I simply turned and began leaving the room before I heard a small giggle coming from behind me. It was then that a horrid sound followed as I could hear a faint whisper being produced by the tiniest voice.

"Benjamin!" the thing whispered.

My heart sank within my chest and I dared not turn myself toward the entity. I was sure that I was being stalked for some nefarious purpose and I did not wish to discover what that purpose would be. Instead, I quietly drew my pistol and began walking toward the door of the bedroom slowly. I once more heard a giggle from the right side of me this time as though the being sat upon the bed beside me.

I could not allow myself to fall for such an attempt at scaring me, but the urge to defend myself took me over. I still managed to fight this and return my gaze to the door as I pushed it against the wall and took a step outside. I then felt the urge to turn to the right and peer down the stairs only to see a host of these shadow beings staring back. I launched myself forward in an attempt to move past them and lock them out of my bedroom.

This, however, was not to be the case as I was pulled back into the guest bedroom and thrown to the ground. I slammed my head upon the wood flooring and had become dazed for a moment. My instincts took over my body anyway and pulled my pistol pointing it toward the door that was now shut. As I waited for these beings to begin their torture, I watched them phase through the wall and door as if they were not there. These beings then formed into an even more distinct shape against the background of the darkness. My lamp had been taken from me and no longer shined but had rolled underneath the bed just behind me.

The beings now stood all around me with the smallest standing atop the bed behind me. It was then that the whispers began, but seemed to resonate from nothingness. I knew that these beings were speaking about me, but did not react to anything nor move. I could hear these whispers without seeing the motions that would be made by a living being. Instead, it was sound that came from stagnant shapes that stood all around me and seemed both real and unreal.

My heart raced ever faster as time passed until I could hear my name being whispered amongst the other words. Nothing else that was said was as clear as this nor was it intelligible.

Now it was that the beings looked down on me immediately and altogether. My heart then seemed to stop beating in my chest as I produced a crucifix from my shirt pocket and wrapped it around my hand. I called out for God to remove these beings, but they did not leave. Rather, they seemed to be entertained by my actions as I could hear more whispering, but they had begun turning their heads as an animal struggling to understand would. I was not sure now why they would be present but I did not have to wonder about such things for very long.

Immediately, the largest of the group extended its darkness toward me as if reaching down to me. I could feel it caress my face and then touch the middle of my forehead with an immediate tingling. I was then taken to an altogether odd place as it seemed that I was in the normal world, but standing within the sky. The world that would be below me, was now above me as I simply stood there. I could then see these beings moving from the clouds below and rising to meet me upon my plane. I did, however, feel invited and warm without the need to run or defend myself. Once more the taller being moved to just in front of me and placed its darkness upon my right shoulder.

"It is returning, he will return, it returns. Protect yourself and your wife now. She needs your help. Be cautious young descendant. Understand that we are everything and nothing. Call upon us within your heart when you falter."

I was then cast from the floor of the sky and tumbled down the long space toward the ground only falling back into my body to find the lamp lit and resting beside me. I breathed in a deep breath while struggling to understand anything that had happened or said at that moment. I was confused, to say the least, but thought it best to simply sleep in my bed. I ventured into my bedroom and removed my clothing only to fall onto the bed and begin dreaming immediately. I could not remember these dreams, however, but a rather deep loathing and hate. It was not unusual for me to feel these things in my dreams, but I never understood what made this happen.

Now I would be taken deeper into my dreams as my psyche seemed to collapse in upon itself until I felt reality within each moment of such a dream. The feeling was odd, to say the least as it was that I was asleep and knew this but my soul resided in a distant place as I watched myself sleep. I could see every motion even in the darkness, but also was allowed to watch the sunrise on another day. My return to my body, however, was not immediate. I lingered in this place until it seemed that I was forced to return. I opened my eyes to barely realize all that had happened as I slept.

I had no visitors to my knowledge on this day and the only person who would visit was away in Europe. I quickly threw the minimum of clothes upon my body and ran to the front door immediately. Upon opening the door, a man stood before me in a brown suit with his head lowered and holding a note toward me. His demeanor was an oddity as well as was his hat upon his head. I only saw a glimpse of his face as he seemed to smile toward me then turn away and walk out of view.

I only knew this to be Mr. Edgar from the train, but he was no longer the same man. That is to say that he held the same face, but his skin was dark now as if he had traveled from the southern states only to be here upon my stoop. My mind wished to make sense of this to say that this man had escaped to his freedom and was now in the employ of Mr. Edgar, but this did not align either. Now it was that I looked away from my stoop and across the street only to see an elder black man who held a stick in his right hand along with a large dark dog beside him. He cackled for a moment and then turned to walk away. I'll admit that I moved from the stoop and began to follow him, but he had vanished completely. I continued to gaze into the distance as Mary approached my side.

"Who was that, my love?" she asked.

"I am not sure my love, but I think that a man I once knew is not who he seemed to be," I replied with a confused tone.

Mary and I returned to the front of the home as I shut the door behind me and then immediately began looking upon the note:

Benjamin,

We are watching and waiting to assist. You know nothing now, but an ocean of vision awaits.

-Mr. Edgar

The only other item was an address that seemed to be somewhere in Georgia which I found to be odd as I had never known anyone in that state. I also had never traveled so far south before, but I would welcome another adventure. Yet I knew not how I would as Mary needed my care and I would not travel so soon after arriving here. I had never witnessed such an event, however. It was then that my mind gave up trying to put pieces together and simply cemented the sight into my inner vision forever.

Such a powerful sighting would haunt my mind and dreams forever, but I knew this was not to scare me. It seemed an empowering sighting of something odd and otherworldly. I was only ready to see this now, however, and truly accept the vision itself. I knew that I was being pulled deeper into the world of the supernatural, but it no longer worried me. I could feel that I had been given the help that I need without understanding it in my mind.

I placed the note into my top pocket and continued into the dining room as Mary emerged from the kitchen with bread and some bacon. I did not know how she would have acquired such things on this morning, but I reasoned that she had visited the grocer as I slept. It was now ten o'clock in the morning as I sat at the table and began eating. My mind was calm now more than it had been before and I was ready to move forward with my life once more. Yet now it would be with caution as it had been foretold that this being would return to haunt me.

The only thing to give me pause was that I had no worries about a demon returning to haunt my life as I just seemed to know what to do. It would be that I would kill it as I would kill any other being. The only difference was that I would be banishing this being back to where it emerged. Any other being would pass to another existence rather than being placed back within its reality. Though something did seem to cause a tinge of pain within my heart whenever I considered these thoughts. I knew that something would change for the worse, but I could not say what it would be. Instead, I brought my focus back to reality and continued eating the food that Mary cooked. It was delicious in every regard as the bread was moist within and crunchy outside. Steam rose from the bread and the bacon whilst butter seemed to melt from the bread and onto my tongue.

The whole of this meal was delicious but simple in every sense and I could not wait for more. I continued eating more than I normally would and then removed myself from the table to finish placing my tie on my neck. I also grasped my new pistol and prepared it for the day while also placing new salt rounds into my older pistol. I then placed the old pistol in a harness on my right side while my new pistol was on the left side of my vest. I knew that everyone would spy my gun upon my side, but I cared not for such worries.

I finished tightening my necktie and straightened my vest before moving downstairs and collecting Mary for a day out. We had both decided now over breakfast to travel to other places within the city. I was eager to take her to such places and allow her mind to absorb the amazing and most interesting sights within the city. I was more than happy to see such a smile on her face as we left our home and moved toward the central portions of New York City. We visited the docks leading out into Hudson Bay along with the many fine colleges within the city. All of our parks were of fine and beautiful stature compared to anywhere else in the world save for Boston. Yet we had seemed to develop a culture that surrounded the austere beauty of landscape and cityscape colliding together to produce many sights that seemed picturesque.

Mary especially appreciated the many statues that dotted the city along with flowers and trees arranged with such care. Our city is unique from anything around the world in every sense of the word.

Yet her heart had been captured still by the roses growing beside Edric's home. Try as I might, I could not capture her imagination in any other way than to return once more to the location where Edric dwelt. Still yet we were able to visit the museums and galleries in our area of the city. I thought it interesting to see such a woman from a plain background viewing these magnificent works of art hanging on the walls of such large galleries. Still, every sight of opulence and fine art could not capture her heart until seeing the gardens. Mary was a woman who appreciated the beauty of the natural world more than any man's creation. This warmed my heart as I could feel the gaze toward the same beauty that had been taken by the great painters and sculptors.

She was a woman tapped into the immense well of inspiration for anyone undertaking an artistic endeavor beyond any other endeavor. The only role for myself within Mary's life at this point was the agent of each view that we could see. The only other prospect that captures Mary would be that of the libraries stationed around the city for anyone to use. The intellectual pursuits undertaken by those who would wish to be surrounded by a wealth of information. I too was enthused by the same attraction but had been inhibited from visiting until now. My work was such that it would take my attention continuously and without stop.

Now it would be that I would have to facilitate better opportunities for those who would wish to work under me. My next stage in life would see me bringing about enjoyment and relaxation for myself and my family. Surely Mary would wish to see more of this world while enjoying comfort. Still, it was my duty to tend to my business and oversee any needs that might arise. I would not be a true businessman unless I was otherwise capable of assisting my employees and their needs.

The day proceeded without interruption until the late hour of six as the summer sun had begun to drop in the sky. Then I found myself sitting in a restaurant of immaculate nature. The name of this establishment did not matter to me in the least so long as the cuisine would continue its smells and flavors. It began that Mary and I wished to enter Delmonico's which I had desired to visit for some time. I would have never entered such a find and opulent place at any other time without company. I was the sort of man who would conspire on business plans alone in a bar. I could not have longed for a more engaged outing than with Mary, however.

I could not long for the days of my youth as I pondered new tasks at the bank for the next day or stayed late in my office to prepare the next morning's ledgers. Such was a life that I had longed for, but have tired of experiencing. I can no longer hold onto such minuscule dreams anymore as I have tired of working for another. I longed to create my own fortunes and find my own wealth within this world. This was the desire from a young age when I had been limited in the number of luxuries I could enjoy.

My family was not poor by any such standards, but we were not of the upper class in society. However, it was the balls that we would attend for military service that became my drive to want such a life every day. I had longed to make wealth for my family that would follow them through the generations. No matter the changes that would be undertaken within the world, we would be able to survive easily. I was not a man who would be satisfied with gold or diamonds, however. I wanted something much more sustainable and that could be used for longer than one life.

This led me to understand that it was my desire for a better life without stately mansions and sprawling estates. Instead, I wanted to live modestly but without any wants not being met. I wished to save the bulk of my wealth rather than squander it on meaningless things. It was my dream to travel the world and see how others would live. To be engaged within the wider realm in which we live and to experience true beauty. Never before would it be more accessible than in a time such as now. Our world had reached a pinnacle of advancement and achievement. This culminated in a time that would allow for worldwide travel upon beautiful steamships. The world was now more accessible than ever before and I wished to take advantage of such things.

Mary and I had begun to drink the wine that had been lovingly poured by our waiter. I was not sure what my stomach wished for the evening, but I was sure that it had everything to do with the steak. I knew that it would be the best cut of meat and the best marbling of the meat. It had been some time since I had been able to enjoy such a fine and delicious cut of meat. I had made it a point that Mary and I would be treating ourselves to the finest for the week. I was simply fortunate within my heart that I had been able to reach this level in my life. The troubles of the past few days had been harrowing, to say the least, but I could not have asked for a time that would teach me more than that. The toughest lessons that I had learned in all my days were those learned in uncomfortable times. I did not wish to attract such evil into my world and bring about a struggle for my sanity. Now it was that I would enjoy the peace of my life without thinking about what other troubles may lie in our future.

Mary and I continued to converse as I looked about the room we had been seated within and took in the fine tablecloths with draperies hanging about the room. Every guest seemed to comple- ment the structure as we were all dressed in the most lavish clothing. The cuisine smelled delicious and was to behold, but I desired to taste my steak for the first time. The carpet throughout the room was beautiful to behold as it added to the colorful space. All around me, I could see crimson and cream complimented in everything. Nothing could have allowed my mind to be placed at ease more than this moment. I could feel that Mary and I had been freed from the evil that threatened every facet of our lives. This darkness would now fade into the distant memory, but the tribulations experienced by Edric and I would linger forever. Though I did hope that these memories would leave me in a shorter period, I could not say for certain. Only time would tell as to whether I would be driven mad by these dark revelations from within my mind.

Mary and I enjoyed our meal with several glasses of wine along with delicious foods and desserts to share between us. We reveled in a manner that we both had wished for since our meeting. I could not have hoped for more fun with Mary on such a lovely and cool night. I could not understand how such a lovely and bright woman would choose a plain man such as myself. Perhaps it was my knack for entertaining Mary with jokes or cynical comments that I would occasionally make.

I did have to admit that my disposition in relation to life itself was bleak at times, but I tried to curb my negative feelings toward such things. It was not that I could not see life through any other lens, I simply felt an appreciation for the dark and macabre aspects of life. I did find myself being carried away with snide yet humorous comments that I had made about a well-to-do woman. Mary did not appreciate it in any measure, but I felt that it had to be said. It was, of course, in poor taste but I saw no harm in it since nothing had been said to the woman. Now it was all that she could do to not laugh at such silly things that I would utter.

Mary and I walked from the restaurant under a moonlit evening along with a host of stars that had begun to shine. The air was peaceful and calm for such a hot day, but it was appreciated. Nothing could have given warnings of strange occurrences or frightening visions that haunted me. I had not felt so free since the day that I met Mary and knew that I could not live without her. She was my partner in everything and the woman who knew me the most.

"Was the meal up to your standards, my love?" I asked.

"It was delicious. I have never tasted such a stew in my life and I will miss it." Mary replied heartily.

She had become a more open and caring woman since her ordeal as it had begun to affect her more than I would have realized. I wished to ease her pain, but I feared bringing it to the surface again. I simply wished that she would feel residual feelings and not remember images of all that she would have witnessed. Tonight, however, we danced along the walks and streets that led us home. The air was crisp with a cool breeze that blew ever softly by. We had come to enjoy such days since the heat of the days both within North Carolina as well as New York. Now it was that Mary and I had reached the stoop of our home as we kissed and fumbled to open the door together. I had resisted her advances at first, but I knew that I would not hold out for long. When we did get the door open, however, we immediately locked it behind us and dashed up the stairs. Mary had enticed me to the bedroom as a spider does a fly. I could not help but follow at the same rate of speed only stopping to remove my clothing. I was never more eager to be with Mary than now as I wished only the best for both of us.

Mary removed her dress as quickly as she could with some assistance from myself. I nearly tripped when removing my pants and placing them upon the dresser. Now it was to be that Mary and I were found under the covering of our bed embracing and kissing gently. We played back and forth as we bit at each other's lips eventually ending with passionate kissing. Our tongues finding each other in a blind frenzy within such a moment of passion and lust. I could not stop myself from taking Mary in my arms and moving my lips down her neck gently. I could not stop myself from caressing her waist in my hands as my lips began a slow descent to Mary's breasts.

I could no longer feel myself but her as well as though two hearts beating as one. Where I ended she began and where she began I ended. Neither of us could understand what we were being driven to do as we had become engrossed in the moment. Mary lifted her breasts to my mouth without hesitation and with all passion in her heart. She held and caressed me as I pulled her nipple into my mouth only to see bumps forming upon her skin. Our caressing became much more graceful while only using our fingertips to stimulate every portion of each other. Quickly our passions had taken over and we had devolved into thrusting and deep undulations of pleasure that erupted throughout the room. I embraced Mary as the woman she was while she tended to every need that a man could understand.

The remainder of the night was uneventful, however, as we simply talked and read books together in our bed. Comfort was bountiful on this night as we welcomed the end of the day by sharing whiskey. We had no other choice but to share one glass between us. The cool breeze from the window rolled into the room and left a slight nip in the air. This ensured that Mary and I would not leave the comfort of our bed for anything short of larceny. We both stayed this way until our eyes began to close and we drifted into the night.

11

The morning came upon Mary and me without issue as it was the most comfortable sleep that I had felt in a long time. We had both awoken together shortly after feeling the warmth of the sun shining into the room. The world outside continued as it had the days before and did not seem different in any way. I knew that I had fallen asleep, but since I had no dream, I was not sure what had happened during the night. Yet I was relieved to have an emptiness within my mind rather than being tormented by otherworldly ideals. Nothing to stress my heart nor to make sweat bead down the side of my face.

I turned to see that Mary would share the same as she awoke without a presence of haste while also showing relaxation upon her face. Her eyes drooped slightly which indicated to me that she was in a peaceful understanding of her morning. I then took it upon myself to move from the bed and begin dressing. The paper was to have arrived shortly before and would allow for the perusing of anything interesting.

By the time this thought was complete, I had placed my ascot around my neck and laced it properly with a gentleman's touch. My mind raced with the possibility that our torment had finally ended. I was sure that Edric would be experiencing the same as well, but hopefully better. I did not know the extent of his travels, but I knew that it would not be simply leisure. Still, the conversations that we would have upon his return would prove fascinating in every sense of the word. I could not understand why a man such as Edric would wish to call any place home.

Now it was that I would move from the bedroom and down the stairs in my usual manner, but I was not sure what would await me upon entering the lower level. My time was to be occupied, however, by the readying of coffee in anticipation of Mary's choice of restaurants for the morning. I could not allow her to continue working in such a manner as this without help in caring for the home. I could make the final move of our new life and begin looking for a maid for our home. I knew that Mary would find issues with this, but it was not to replace her. Instead, it was this time for me to bring some amount of ease about caring for our home.

My second course of action for the day was that of visiting the construction office and beginning renovations upon the bank. I only had to give the word toward the confirmation and payment of the project to begin the project within the next month. I was sure that the resources would have to be collected while working to free a work crew from other areas. Our city was growing quickly and without tire as more people had begun moving into the area. People of all backgrounds visited the city but it was the main grouping of Irish who had left their homes for our burgeoning city.

Time would only tell what position the flood of new citizens would hold within our city, but the only hope I would have is for their success within our city. The only issue that truly saddened me was the sight of worsening conditions for new arrivals on our lands. Though I know that this must happen given those who would rule the city in the least proper way. Prejudices against those who would arrive and take space from those already here have become all-consuming and beyond belief. I could not tell the horrors that I had witnessed in my time studying within the city, but it had profoundly changed my mind. Where I had once not given care to those issues, I am now engaged in the idea of allowing these people to provide for themselves.

Mainly it could be seen that the Irish have held no wealth when selling all they owned to arrive upon free soil. Many would have known of the issues affecting Ireland in these days that would bring about such migrations. Yet it was that such people were to cooperate with the needs of the city when arriving in a foreign nation and sticking to regulations to remain. It would not be fortuitous to arrive in such a land with a hungry family to be returned to the poverty that you had desired to flee. It would be now that immigrants would seek the wealth and immaculate nature of America not to leech from the rest, but to make a way for themselves.

Now it was that I would bring work to such a business within the city that had become owned and run by Irish who know nothing more than construction. Yet I would be lauded by anyone wishing for me to search for a more traditional company with which business should be done. Though this would be regardless of lowered prices in relation to more long-standing companies. I did, however, see many demonstrations of construction techniques utilized by such a company and found it to be superior for the amount of money I would spend.

Eventually, Mary emerged from the upper level and joined me in a cup of coffee along with our usual morning banter starting from my reading of the newspaper. Mary enjoyed the gradual emergence of her mental faculties from the fog that lingered after an intense and deep slumber. Our rare sharing of this blackened refreshment seemed to do much for arousing Mary's mood and bringing out a more apparent focus from her.

The one thing that stood out as different on this morning was that Mary and I had no desire for food and so decided that we would attend to my errands instead. We set out sights toward the work mill of my chosen construction company, O'Brian and Sons Construction. Normally I would have to consult with the clerk within the headquarters just outside the city, but recent long-term work orders had allowed for a temporary location within the city. If the work was steady enough to warrant such a location then it was in good under-standing that the quality of their work would be magnificent.

Perhaps it was my frugal mentality or the research that I had conducted several months before my departure to the southern states, but I was sure this would be a cost-efficient and better move. I wished the bank to receive a more than modest improvement to attract new business to the location. So it was that O'Brian and Sons would allow for such improvements in a timely and cost-efficient manner. I trusted their methods and judgments as well as being able to change orders while knowing these changes will be met.

It would be a short project but would require intense focus from myself and allow me to depart my home for most of the work days. Such an idea was also attractive to Mary as she would, no doubt, wish to come with me and see more of the city. I could not abide her wandering throughout the city alone as there had been more seedy communities popping up throughout the area. I could not allow my wife of good standing and gentle character to be taken advantage of within the confines of such communities. This was not to say that I would not mingle with such people, but that I would wish to be present and accompany Mary through these areas. Immediately we left our home and entered a taxi as it moved slowly down the street in front of our home. The motion was smooth and easy from the horses that pulled the taxi through somewhat crowded streets.

Our city thrived on moving forward with ideas and decisions quickly and without delay as much as possible. So it would be that our day saw many vying for attention from patrons with the best and most opulent structures in which to do business. Now it was that I would attempt to bring the attention of other investors and moguls to see the Northeast Bank as a vibrant and renewed business. Surely these men would wish to bring their money to our bank to invest their savings and business holdings. Every thought such as these made my heart jump with a joy that I did not understand, but the excitement of business was attractive nonetheless.

I could not understate the length of time that it took for our taxi to move slowly through the city to our location. It was now that I could see that the current project for this construction company was to restore a church to a much better state than the current. Craftsmen and architects moved throughout the yard attempting to pull lumber and resources to be built into the structure. Mary and I were amazed at such a process and stood for a moment to admire the amount of work and artistry going into the project.

We also discussed the heat of the day and how it seemed to not affect these men in any way as they ran to and fro. The foremen wondered the yard and observed the movements of each person running about and yelling out orders to those working on the structure. I could never imagine working in such a way but had instead focused on the life of a clerk for several years. I had found there to be a fulfilling life from such a humble profession but knew that I held no affinity to work with wood or stone to build anything.

Mary and I entered the office of the site to speak with the work master and present the ideas to him. Immediately the clerk seemed to look upon Mary with hesitation, but said nothing more than, "How can I help you sir?"

I did not say anything at first then introduced myself and Mary to the man while requesting to speak with the work master for a new project. This was met with slight derision from the clerk along with hesitation to promise such a meeting. After a moment of convincing he held out his hand toward the work master's door.

I knocked upon the work master's door only for him to yell out, "Ya! Enter sir!". I motioned to Mary for her to follow as I opened the door and entered the room. We both took our seats as the man seemed to question Mary's presence with his eyes.

"I have come to present a work order to you as we had spoken of in January. Are you still agreeable to the terms we had set?" I asked.

He began speaking only stop as he looked upon Mary for a second time.

"Is there something troubling you sir?" I asked.

"Nothing Mr. Price! Though I find it to be in poor taste to bring a woman into our work yard. I was under the impression that you would come alone." Mr. O'Brian replied.

"If you find issue with my wife being present then it would be in my best interest to no longer employ your company. I need work done not superstitious beliefs lingering within our deal. My wife is present because I asked her to be present nothing more or less. Shall I move my interests to your competitors?" I replied.

Mr. O'Brian moved his focus back to me and shook his head as I laid a list of items that I needed modeled during the project terms. Only a moment had passed for the work master to read the list and nod his head. He then produced a piece of paper and a quill to jot some notes upon this piece of paper and then returned my list.

"It will be a few months before we will be able to send an architect to your bank and begin work. I am sorry to say that our current projects have not gone according to plans. We will have to close our current work before we can entertain another project." He stated. I said nothing more and nodded as he scribbled a cost ledger for the work to get started then handed me the paper.

With that, I stood from my seat and showed Mary out of the room as I thanked Mr. O'Brian for his cooperation. Mary and I left the office as I bade the clerk good day to only have the same said back to us. I could not say that it was the Irish in general who held this belief or that it was a stigma that came with the business of contracting. I did not, however, feel that I was agitated or angry that Mr. O'Brian would act in such a manner toward Mary. I was simply letting it be known that I would not stand for anyone to treat her in that manner.

I may not be a famous man, but I am never going to allow the good standing of my wife be diminished in such a manner. She was more than just my wife after all that we had faced and I could feel my heart growing more fond of her. I felt more in a partnership now than a situation relegating us to the man of the house and lady of the home. We were more than that now and more important to each other in every sense of the thought. Mary would be just as important as myself as she would be able to conduct business in my stead.

Though this was not the traditional way in our world, I would not allow for anyone outside of my own family to deal with my holdings in my place if I were able to do so. I did not wish to alienate

anyone within any deal that I would make, but mutual and benefi-
cial respect is a calling that many would not understand. This is all
to say that I would not normally send Mary in my stead, however,
but there is a great chance that she would last beyond my own
demise. I could not know anything beyond that point save for the
holdings within this world that would wear my name. In such an
event, Mary then our children would become stewards of the legacy
that I am starting now.

Now it would seem that we left the yard only for a call of my
name to ring out over the breeze that wafted through the air. It was
faint, yet recognizable in so many ways save for the identity of the
voice. I could feel a cold chill that enveloped my position within the
area as well as all senses that I could use to detect anything. It was
this feeling that began driving my mind, desires, and reactions as I
turned to witness a deformed hag. She was hunched slightly with
skin that seemed to leak a manifestation of evil upon the ground. I
feared that she might start toward me, but she simply stood there
with a wide and jagged smile upon her face.

I could see that she was slowly losing her skin as it slumped from
her frame only to squish upon the ground. This left fingers of bone
reaching out toward me as she began moving forward toward Mary
and myself. I had fallen into a predicament as I was reduced to a
nervous mess. I also could not alert anyone as to these happenings as
I feared that I would be labeled as unwell and taken to Witherbrook
myself. This certainly could not happen in any capacity nor could I
produce a firearm in public to strike a charge.

Instead, I grasped Mary's hand firmly and strode toward the side
of the street quickly and in a stiff manner. My stance was that of a
man knowing that he would miss out on an event or meeting at high
noon. Now I would be sure to not look behind me for fear that this
being would be called to action against my physical form. Upon
reaching the street, I stood helpless with Mary at my side as I could
hear a breathing beginning to come closer to my place. Stopping in
place I was a pale and rigid figure while still maintaining my stance
with Mary's hand clutched tightly in mine. I would not allow them to

take her or I within an abyss of darkness and fog nor would I fall victim to losing my life to something so unholy.

It was then that I turned to look behind me as I could no longer hear or see anything. I breathed a sigh of relief for a moment then flashed a smile toward Mary only to realize that I could feel a presence behind me. It grasped the back of my pants while working its bony grasp up my legs and back until I felt a firm grasp as it mounted itself upon my shoulders and then pulled upward. I could see nor hear anything, but feel something climbing me stubbornly and slowly in the most alarming manner. The imprints of feet stiffening upon my back and bringing pressure with it as this being became more real by the moment.

Only now was the breathing of this creature becoming known to my hearing once more as a wheezing sound could be faintly heard. Somehow a damp and clammy sensation dropped upon me until the taxi pulled directly in front of me. My instinct was to board the vehicle as quickly as possible and take a seat wherever I could find it. Surely being surrounded by people would make this horrid thing dissipate back to the ether from which it came. The last of the happenings being a whisper in my right ear along with the sensation of a gooey tongue liking the edge of my neck.

"He has risen for you my nephew and I will usher you into his grasp. It will either be you or the Colombian whore you call a wife. Wish for satan, but be taken by more."

The whisper then faded into the distance and was gone once more as the sounds of the taxi wheels clacking upon the street rushed to me. Mary said nothing in this moment but could tell that something profound had occurred while not calling attention to it. I suspected that she knew what had happened and may have experienced the same while being in the clutches of this darkness. God could only stop such hideous frightful uttering from nothing detectable. I took a deep breath and held onto the cross that I held in my left shirt pocket. My mind had been flooded with a haze that had dulled the sharpness of my usual thoughts.

Now it was that I had been struck mute and dumb in the worst way imaginable as everyone around me suspected nothing of my plight. This thought passed as Mary grasped my hand and pulled me from the taxi and onto the street. It was now that a weight had lifted from my body and a scream emanated from all around me. My breath had been leeched from my chest leaving me doubled over and gasping for relief. I knew nothing of this being only to say that it was my aunt and one of the faces that protruded from the last sighting of this demon. She was a foul and twisted sort now as she had been taken to her proper fate.

I would not bring shame and hate upon my family, but my mother and aunt could nevermore be considered anything but evil. No matter the situation, when one gives themselves to evil then they are damned to their fate. Salvation shall never find the wicked as they are bent to the will of stifling malice. I was sure now that their souls had been infested and perverted in the worst manner for any living thing. They had been assimilated into the collective that had inhabited this void between worlds. I feared for any memories that Mary would obtain from this place in time as it would be too painful and horrid to remember.

I caught my breath in time to step onto our stoop and then move swiftly into our home with Mary pulling my arm the entirety of the way.

"What has happened Benjamin? I know that you have been seeing things and I want to know about them." She stated with a forceful demeanor.

It only took a moment of gazing into Mary's beautiful eyes to begin sharing any and all information that I could. At first, I began slowly only for the impatient look upon her face to grow more distinct with every passing moment. This all served to give me the sensation that I had become a scolded child waiting for his mother to spank him. Instead, we spent several hours talking about the happenings of North Carolina and the journey here. I also included all that had happened leading to and inside the asylum with Edric.

Mary stood now with a shocked look upon her face as she seemed to process everything that was stated. After some moments she replied to my statements with a deep and labored breath.

"I wish to be angry with you for not telling me everything that had happened sooner, but it would never help our situation. I am not as rational as you, my love, and I give into my emotions but you have told me the truth and I value that. You are a bastard in every sense of the word for withholding this information. I cannot blame you. You care for me and protect me with such love and care so I will return this to you. How can I help you, my love?" Mary asked.

I could never have expected Mary to respond in such a way, but she had captured my interest and respect. She was resilient, to say the least, and seemed to understand and absorb these happenings without becoming overly emotional. I could feel that she had reached a point of exhaustion with the ordeal since North Carolina and now it was never more visible. I had suspected that she knew more than she would admit, but I had come to understand that I told myself this to comfort my mind. I did not wish to deceive Mary, but the projection that I would be easing her mind more to hide these things from her could never be more of a mistake than now.

"I am sorry my love. I did not wish to hide such things from you nor did I wish any harm to come to you. I lost pieces of myself in the battles to protect you and our home. Though now I ask myself what it was worth. My love for you is never ending and will endure all as long as I no longer taint it with these deceptions. Forgive me my love and allow me another fading chance to heal your trust for me."

Mary knew nothing but love for me at this moment while also allowing herself to trust me and any words I could speak. This was followed by a passionate embrace finished by a deep and loving kiss. I could never have words for the depth of grace that Mary held in all things nor could I wish to taint that again. Because of this under-standing, Mary stated that she had learned much from her dreams since her possession. She informed me that it was iron that did damage to this entity along with another compound that seemed to be much less explosive. Instead, it seemed to burn with an intense glimmer of green fire as if being from Hell itself. I could not understand this in any measure but retained the understanding of bringing iron against such beings. This was information that I did not need necessarily, but I was sure that it would come into use in the future.

This moment finished and was followed by sitting alone in the dining room and smoking a pipe from the corner of my mouth while thinking intently. Mary had begun cooking once again as the clanging and knocking of pans against all manner of surfaces could be heard. I was now faced with the idea that I would have to bring this all to an end. Mary had been introduced to such a dark life and I knew that together we could end this being and its reign of terror. I would no longer shoulder such burdens without the aid of my lovely and capable wife. Yet I would not invite her in place of Edric given her sensitive and innocent nature. Never would I wish her to have memories of the things spoken or brought about within the dark realm.

So the evening progressed until we both enjoyed a lovely meal and a relaxing evening together. I could feel that Mary and I had reached a consensus that this being was mounting another assault upon our family and home with intense rage. This was to unnerve us and throw us into a doubting and melancholy mood that we would never be beyond its grasp. Though I doubted this entirely as I felt that this was all a bluster to steal the joy and light from our lives only to torment us forever. I would never allow this nor would Mary be complicit in such torment without meeting death first. I had become fond of her attitude in this way as we had needed to hold fast to the values and understandings that brought peace to our lives.

The sun faded below the horizon in a magical display of colors that no one could reproduce only to reveal bright and beautiful stars hanging within nothingness. Mary and I found ourselves sitting on the porch and trading stories about the oddities that we had witnessed. She spoke of being forms within the wood on the edge of her family's farm that seemed to hide just beyond the light. She stated that any torch that had been brought to bear upon the trees during these sightings would reveal nothing. It was as though these forms could not be seen in the light yet manifested within the deeper darkness.

Eventually, I began sharing the events of my childhood and odd things that I would witness around my home as well. Forms of soldiers lurking about in odd places within the small town that sprang up around the military forts we had lived near. Witnessing young men being visible then fading to nothingness before your very eyes along with screams. Nothing could have compared to the events of our recent history as it was that we were being pursued to no end. I would have rather witnessed a spirit every morning rather than the feeling of being absorbed into another realm entirely. This was true fear in my mind as it would come to be that we would vanish from this world without explanation.

In some manner, it felt as though we were sitting on the edge of life and clinging to what little stability we had. This was being done with a sense of camaraderie between Mary and myself, but also brought a feeling of isolation. This was the sickness that lingered in every facet of our lives now and seemed to be a warning call that our time was growing short. Now we waited in the darkness for some-thing to grasp at us and take our whole selves into death. I would never wish to vanish in such a way or fade from this world with such questions and mystery. But it would be this that would be brought to bear if we gave into our demise.

Yet all I could understand and see within this special moment was Mary's smile as I kissed and embraced her in every moment. We would relish our time together and speak of humorous moments when we had first met and the feelings that accompanied them. I was never more ready to die than here in her arms and loving embrace, but I would never succumb without a fight. Mary seemed to share the same sentiment, but fear held no sway over her thoughts and laughter within his moment. We found our raw love and passion that had been fleeting in the days before while forming a bond that neither of us had ever felt.

It was this feeling that gave me the understanding that we were beings without borders only living to intertwine with each other. She was a woman who had faced much hardship while I was a man who had brought myself up to the success that I was now. It was this feeling of tapping into the roots of our being that seemed to take the world away. We were a part of something more and greater while being brought into each other as simple people with desires and wants. It was the perfect moment to allow our minds to see the importance of our survival and love together. Now only the feeling of our hearts bursting together in a symphony of passion, intrigue, and romance.

I could only bring these words to bear upon paper with my own blood being pressed into the pours. The very lifeblood of our romance being that immersion into each other and the worlds and conditions that spawned us. Mary was an amazing woman and I was determined to fight for her at all costs as the vines that bound us together grew into the flesh that was our hearts. I had become her and she had become me along with our thoughts and desires without limits of consequences. Love had taken a strong hold over us in this moment of reflection as we realized that we were beings called into existence for each other and without consideration for any other interactions. Only now could the immensity of the world and our place within it be understood as we stepped beyond our physical selves and into the warm and loving embrace of each other's hearts. I love Mary with my whole being and this had never been more understood than now.

12

The evening ended in a lovely dinner that had been provided to us by Mary's hand. Her affinity for cooking had shown through in every measure of the statement. I had not tasted such a balanced and flavorful stew from any other source. Though upon questioning her profusely on the recipe for the meal, she would not provide any explanation or reason. Still, I was thankful for a wholesome and light dinner as we discussed our desires for the future of our relationship. I could not understand why, but my stomach had felt a resistance to this conversation and its conclusion. It was not as though I would never wish to continue being married to Mary which confused my more logical sensibilities.

The normal activities for the night had fallen way to Mary sitting upon my lap in the front parlor and sharing a bowl of tobacco together. She was a hearty smoker which gave me pause in the beginning, but I felt it proper to not ask. Mary had shown that she could smoke just as we as any man, but with more art to it than gusto. She did not merely blow the smoke about the room but filtered it in such a way as to create different patterns and shapes. I found this to be an extraordinary sight to behold as Mary continued to perform.

Ultimately it would be the description of sharing a pipe with her brothers whilst still on the farm in North Carolina and her country tutelage that brought about this understanding. Yet still, the respect that I held for such a hearty, but beautiful woman grew and grew on that night. Surely it would be that Mary and I would be able to share our notions of the world together as well as our interests. Though I would not allow her to become this person in public unless she willed it to be. I knew that Mary had been taught by the elder women within her family to be this proper lady at all times and not allow for such an un-lady-like persona.

Our smoking culminated in Mary bringing glasses of whiskey for us both to enjoy as we continued to share moments together. Even if those moments were simply sipping whiskey and looking at each other in a flirtatious manner. However, one topic lingered that Mary nor I would wish to share as we had finally achieved our escape from such a topic. This avoidance did not last for long as the sounds of a strange and whistling breeze blew through the outer door that led to the back porch. There was no natural cadence to the noise, but more like someone intentionally whistling into the air.

This was followed by a chill that crept through the back door and into the sitting room until it surrounded Mary and myself. I could feel her skin begin to crawl as I held her tightly against my body as we smoked and talked.

"Why is there a chill Benjamin? Does the summer hold such a chill in the night?" She asked.

I simply shook my head and said nothing for a moment as I waited for another passing of cold air. I could feel nothing, but I had more layers upon my body with Mary's body and my clothing blocking the air. I could, however, believe her as my right ear had felt a slight tingle of coldness that had infected my skin. This was an unusual feeling as it seemed to move about the room as though coming from an entity rather than a weather event. I could not understand it, but I also could not ignore that this was happening to both of us. This led me to convince Mary to come with me to the upper level while closing off the house to the outside world.

Fear had not begun to creep into our home, however, as there had been no escalation of the issue given that we had removed ourselves. Instead, there came a calm that seemed to engulf our home and our bedroom to allow Mary and I to continue enjoying our company. So it was that Mary and I spent meaningful time together within our bed, but without the physical nature of our love. Mary wrapped her arms around me and accepted the love that I would offer with no return attached. She gave me all of the kissing and love elegant affection that I could handle within this moment.

The eventual culmination of our time together was to begin moving for a more carnal lust rather than such an innocent method. Though the time would not allow for such pleasures as it was that a loud wrapping came upon the back door of our home. This was something that had never happened previously and gave rise to the most unsettling feeling within our bodies. Mary paused immediately and turned her head to listen closely as the sounds continued. It was that the knocking came within threes and no other timing. I felt the malice and intent of harm growing within the air once more as I listened in.

Eventually, the sounds moved to a strong force rattling the back door so vigorously that it began shaking the walls that had been attached to the back of the home. Mary withdrew closer to me and pulled the covering over her tighter against her body. I, on the other hand, moved from the bed and took possession of my pistols. Nothing would inflict itself upon my home in such a way without my inspection or defense. Within a moment I had moved to the bottom level and began inspecting the outer reaches of the home through the side windows of the back door. I saw nothing and no form that would be lent to a lunatic threatening my home in the dark.

Instead, my mind raced with the possibility that this was the return of evil upon my home. I dashed back from the door as a new set of beatings upon the door came in wave after wave. Yet I would stand firm, waiting for someone to identify themselves, but without calling upon this force to show itself. I had it firm within my mind that I would surely invite this suffering upon Mary and I once more. I also dare not open the door and allow for the acceptance of any contract that had not been stated. Still, the banging sounds continued for another round until I looked through the window again.

Nothing was revealed through this move again as I decided upon a more stubborn move than to give in and left the door rattling upon its hinges. I returned to Mary within our bedroom and took up the cause of comforting her in this moment of fright.

"I do not know who would call upon us at this hour, but there is no form that I can see, my love," I stated to Mary.

"I can feel something is not right, Benjamin! It has returned for both of us once more my love. We cannot allow this to happen again!" Mary exclaimed.

"I am certain of this my love, but we have little choice but to ignore such disturbances until the morning light."

This did not seem to be a satisfactory answer to Mary as she voted to remain hidden within our bed for the moment. I, on the other hand, had finished cowering to such forces long ago and instead took my place beside her as I began closing my eyes and preparing for sleep. It was then that Mary had urged me to close the window that was beside me for her safety. This was something that I adamantly refused as we would surely roast in the warmth of the summer night.

Instead, I held her close and allowed her to snuggle under my arm so as to hide from the fright that she felt deep within. I could understand this as I had felt the same in previous times, but would no longer allow such emotions to overtake me. I simply blew upon the lamp which stood on the bedside table then lowered my body back under the sheets. I felt that it had not been a long time before I had begun to fade from the waking world. I found myself waking in a dream of the same world that I had just escaped. Though this version of the world had become darker while only being lit by a soft moonlight that filtered into the room.

Now a mist had begun to form outside the open window as it began to move into the room through the open window. This was to only begin moving into the shape of a lovely and elegant woman. The form was white and non-threatening in any way as it moved gracefully across the flooring and to the bed. I could now feel soft hands caressing my cheek as if enticing me to remove myself from the bed. Then came a gentle motion until the entity had sat upon the edge of the bed just a little away from my head.

"Benjamin, wake and speak with me!" The form whispered.

I did as was requested of me albeit slowly and more cautiously than I normally would. Upon sitting upright beside the being, I could feel a loving caressing upon my back from a small and soft hand.

"I have come to guide you, Benjamin. We are calling you home to be with us for eternity. God has allowed for your rest from such a hard life."

"I have felt no discomfort in this life, spirit. Reveal the nature of your visit and how this offer would come." I replied.

"There is an offer from God for you to join your aunt and me in heaven." She whispered.

"Would it not be that my father would call upon me as well?" I asked.

"Your father is being left from this offer as it may want to bring to this place of peace and relaxation. Your time has been completed so come now with me Benjamin and rest in the bosom of God the father!"

"I apologize, Mother, if you are my mother. I will rebuke this offer as my time is not accomplished until I say that it has been completed. I know that this offer is nothing more than the same illusion that guided your evil and greedy hands. Why offer blood and horror for most of my time since seeing you then offer peace and relaxation? I will not be a pawn within this game and I will resist your demon lord. Leave me in this place if your intent is peace." I finished as I climbed back under the covering.

I could now see that the head of this entity had faded into the darkness behind it. This seemed to form a black shroud that partially hid the intent and soul of this form from my vision.

"Be gone with you, Mother. You betrayed father and now me."

These words were not met with another offer or argument but silence as the form had begun to change. Darkened strips of a jelly substance had begun moving all around the form and eventually engulfed it. Now it was that a black gooey form sat upon the bed just away from me while still staring intently in my direction.

I could now feel a shift in the intent of this being and its "offering" as the room seemed to grow darker and more threatening. The voice of such a being had now shifted to being gravelly and unhinged in its enunciation of usual statements and words.

"We will devour you and your pretty "wife" within the void." It said.

I, however, would not entertain such a statement as I spoke forcefully and bade it a good night. This did little to remove the darkness from the entity while also ensuring that this being continued to linger.

"You will be given unto torment in your final hours, Benjamin! Mark our declaration."

With these words, the being left my room while peace and silence took their place again. I fell into sleep once more as my soul raced through the sky and toward the moon. I could feel the world all around me and the darkness that grew upon the face of the Earth. Stillness had been replaced with roaring malice that seems to engulf all that it touched.

I felt the understanding of the universe within me once more and a knowledge that this powerful few were selling our world to darkness. The void had grown stronger and more prevalent now as the intention came about to devour our world with hate and evil. Darkness fell upon the sky as fires raged beneath me but no smoke reached these heights. Screaming and pain filled the night air as animals could not be seen moving about the forests below. I had now embarked upon a journey as time had begun advancing upon the world around me and civilization grew. It had culminated in the vision of a world that would give rise to panic and lunacy as the masses had been coerced by the governments of a dying world. Fools rose to positions of power while those who promised to defend civil justice sold the poor out to slavery in a different manner.

Wonders had come to replace all dignity within every man's heart and weakness of the species fell upon our great nation. America had fallen to the plans of horrid actions from evil men who preyed upon the less fortunate and weak. Madmen dressed as women and women as men until there could be seen no difference. The world crumbled from its foundations as those who held insanity within their minds influenced a world being devoured. The void had come to spread its chaos upon a vilified people who simply tried to conjecture over important matters. Truly the world needed to be prevented from this state and it seemed as though I was being called to action through this vision.

It all began with myself and my family as I would be the one to bring about reason once more. Yet my heart shrank from the desire to save the world while instead allowing for the common man or woman to hold freedom again in the future. *Who would have estimated the darkness within the human heart and the will to condition children to such suffering?* We could never inherit the world in such a manner and we would never be able to sustain it as such. I did not wish to fight the world or the void still yet. I would have to witness and have the removal of something that I loved dearly for my mind to engage in such actions. I was not a warrior and would never pretend to be such. Yet I was dealing with a matter that seemed to be leading to the inevitable destruction of the world.

I will admit to myself that I had become too comfortable in this life as I had begun to achieve everything that I had wanted for myself. Though I had not dove completely into such a life that I would be willing to disregard everything for comfort. I knew that deep within my heart, I would be called to take action and fight for something greater. It would not be the glamour that I relegated to my descendants, but a struggle against forces that I could not comprehend. Though I did not realize that such struggles would be against other-worldly foes altogether. I would achieve such a balance within my life at the loss of something cruel and great as this demon that haunted my home.

The night passed without any further events, but I had felt myself being aloft for some time only to return to my body at first light. I awoke with these memories, but I could not process nor comprehend the understanding that I had once held. My physical self seemed to interrupt such intelligence that would be outside my own. Now reason and science crept back into the cracks between images and tried to account for everything that had been witnessed. That is to say until I had moved past such futile attempts at reason and simply accepted what was and not what is. The world before me immediately became smaller once more and the universe could be forgotten once more.

Such comforts would not last for long, however, as Mary stirred and checked all directions within our bedroom for any malign beings. She no longer held fear within her eyes, but a hatred that I had never witnessed coming from Mary. She had finally reached the point of hating all that our lives had become. She had renounced her victimhood in the eyes of darkened entities that would wish nothing more than control and harm upon her. Mary shined like a light in the darkness that threatened us once more. I could feel her wishing to be done with these moments of fear and falling into sleep wondering if it would be her last waking event.

Mary had found this reaction much quicker than had I, but I welcomed this change in her as I knew that she would be willing to fight alongside me. She was no frail woman nor was she incapable of inflicting harm, but a gentle and happy woman. Yet it seemed when this had been removed from her grasp the animal within herself awoke ready to fight. I could see the huntress shown from within as though a projection of her true and unhindered self. Immediately she jumped from the bed and dressed with a silent focus that seemed to engulf her sense of protection. I loved this side of her and wished nothing more than to see it for myself. Such love would eventually bleed through in an off-putting way for Mary as I would show a much more romantic and connected side of myself. She was the woman of strength that I had longed for and had never known until now. It was this constant learning about her and whom she would wish to be that continued our love beyond the flesh and into the cosmos beyond. I meant for her and she meant for me in a pairing that had been divinely inspired. I craved to feel this as we moved through the beginning of our day.

Breakfast was accented by longing stares into each other's eyes as though we had just begun our courtship. A gentle and persistent need for an embrace or a longing looks that we would wish to find in each other at any moment. Yet when it finally happened, we relished it and committed such a sight to memory for the longer term. The universe could not hold us within a mold but break and crack with each move that Mary and I made forward in our lives. She a beautiful and vibrant creature who longed for love, passion, and caressing. I am a rigid and rooted man who longed to be held in the limelight for just long enough and have wealth backing every desire I held.

Our walking in the park held even more of such expressions as others around us seemed molested by the feeling of such unyielding love. I could see that we infected the world around us with such romance that others had taken to embracing as well. Still, now we would be comfortable in the fact that nothing would bother us as long as we stood firm in our resolutions together. Our life together had become unashamed and unwavering in the face of those who would wish to cast despair and fear toward it. Mary was to me as breathing is to all living creatures upon this earth and I could not understand anything otherwise.

We moved through the greenery all around us as we moved hand in hand for everyone to see our passions bleeding through against the summer heat. We had begun to show beauty as we had begun to bloom together like a rare flower within its display. Yet we could not be captured for any moment or whim of another. We remained upon the ledge of the lofty mountain of passion and romance that they would hold so dear. I had become comfortable in all things divine as I stared into her beautiful hazel eyes until I had lost myself. She felt me from every emotion that I could muster and passed through my heart. We were the vines intertwined in the magnificence of life itself.

I could not understand if it was due to the fact of what we had faced or the promise of what hardships were yet to come. Yet we were compelled to desire each other in these moments as the world would take life from us at any moment. The fight would be long and arduous, to say the least, but together we would be prepared. Our hearts were attached at this moment and no reason could come between such longings with any doubts. We knew that in a short time we would stare death in the eyes and take our lives back from the hindrance that sought to drag us under.

We rounded the last leg of the park and began moving another grove of trees as the sun hung high over our heads. Conversations that we held with each other seemed to be more than just words. It was that we had begun to feel each other as beings that encompassed more than flesh and bone. Mary and I had begun understanding each other as higher beings pressed upon by a world that was not ready for the intensity of our light. Though now we would show this light without any regard for another's feelings toward it. Should it be that someone or something would wish to tarnish such love was beyond us, but still not affecting our current state of being.

Beyond these trees, we moved behind a fountain that across from which sat a statue of a lion that was magnificent to behold. The whole of the location seemed removed and restricted from view due to the bushes around it. Quickly I found myself embracing Mary passionately and without losing eye contact. I kissed her vigorously and without hesitation or regard for anyone around us. Her legs became weak as she began to slide down the statue slowly and unable to fight her urge to collapse. I did not hesitate to embrace her emotions, love, and sense of being as I held her close and continued kissing Mary hungrily.

She began to unfold and relax with each passing moment as I continued to passionately love her in seclusion from those around us. She was the flower and I had become the man simply trying to take advantage of her love while stabilizing her all the same. The colors of the world blended around us as I held her close while commanding her lust to writhe within her. The summer heat faded from our feeling as the world bled away and left only our love to behold at that moment. The fears associated with being caught within this moment by another melted away as well as we concentrated on bringing each other to a conclusion. Nothing would stop the passions from flowing from one being to another and the love that accompanied the embrace that we shared. Moment after moment passed as we continued in this way until an explosion of sensations could be felt between our physical selves. Mary had bloomed once more in the later stages of romance as I had resisted my own urges in favor of a more intimate setting.

We had both become the only beings within this moment as I lowered her to the ground and allowed her to adjust her clothing. I simply blocked her womanhood from being on display for all to see within the park. The world flooded back into my mind as we resumed what we had begun moments before and moved along the path again. I could never have hoped for more or less than this love as the fear of what we had done returned to our hearts. Restrictions of the world became more prevalent within our minds and we simply wished that everything had happened in a hidden manner. The only thing left to observe in these following moments was that of the sensations of the summer returning to tired bodies ready to engage in more.

Mary and I resolved to shop for the few groceries needed in the wake of an immeasurably romantic day. We then returned to our domicile for rest and to enjoy ourselves in a more intimate and private setting up on the back porch. Now it was that we had been left to our whims within these moments and without regard for any other. We made the move to drink our whiskey and smoke together until retiring to the dining room for another activity. The speech had no place within this moment as our embracing and melding of spirits continued over and over throughout the day until the evening had come to pass. When we had tired of the table, we moved to the sitting room and then to the bedroom in the late evening for cooler air.

Mary and I had become much more comfortable with each other and without the restrictions of clothing or other such coverings. I could not be certain that any other would have heard the sounds of such heated engagements, but I was sure that they would say nothing. I could not have held care as long as Mary did not stop such enjoyment out of fear or hesitation. Instead, we stopped ourselves from further enjoyment as fatigue had begun to take us and we moved to clothe ourselves once more. We made our final position on the porch and partook in the activity of smoking again. It was a repeating pattern but was nonetheless the whims of our inner desires for our day.

13

The evening came upon us faster than I could have understood as Mary and I shared such wondrous moments. I was smitten in a manner more powerful than anything I had ever felt, but there seemed to be an unsettling aura that lingered over our home now. The events of last night had moved beyond the edge of my memory as Mary and I found ourselves finishing dinner on the back porch. Many memories had coalesced in meeting each other over and over on this porch which gave this location a magical feeling. My heart grew heavy, however, as I knew that the night would approach and I would not see Mary until morning.

Every moment that passed seemed to drag my soul closer to isolation within my own mind as I soared to interesting and distant lands. Yet a chill moved over the area swiftly as I had taken the last taste of the stew that Mary had made for us. The warmth that filled my stomach did little to stave off the chill that lingered across my flesh. Mary immediately grasped her arms as she shivered in her seat. I offered her my coat from inside the home, but she declined this offer. I knew that she would warm within the moment and all would be right again as we sat hand in hand on the porch. Our chairs creaked in the summer heat as the chill faded to a subtle wind that gently kissed my cheeks.

I could not understand how this was possible in the dead of summer, but I felt it best to not ponder. Instead, my senses had been met with a foul odor that lingered from inside the home as I could hear a crashing sound. I asked Mary to remain in her chair as I moved inside the home to look about for an intruder. Subsequently, I found nothing but an empty home that held the warmth of the day within. There was only silence now as the world moved about outside the front windows of our home. No one had reacted as though they heard anything from the street whilst I placed these thoughts in the back of my mind.

Instead, I moved to the back porch and took my seat once more to talk with Mary. I produced my pipe from my vest pocket as I had done a thousand times and began puffing away on a fresh bowl of tobacco. Mary joined as she could but seemed to still feel the icy grasp upon her being. I could not understand how this was still lingering in the air, but Mary seemed to be uncomfortable as I offered her my coat for the second time. If I had not felt the creeping chill then I would relegate the matter to her body feeling something that wasn't there. Still yet, I would not doubt her feeling at this moment, but I had no longer been allowed to feel such things.

She then looked toward me for a moment until I returned my attention to her eyes as she explained that she felt something off in the air. I tried to rationalize this feeling, but Mary refuted any arguments that I would raise with her. She left me in a manner to investigate the home once more as I feared that she would be feeling what had happened to her before. I did not wish to waste my time, but I had to take this seriously as she had been possessed once already. Immediately I moved to our bedroom and produced some charges from my chest of drawers then placed them within my pockets. I could feel the same sinister air that lingered now and I did not wish for it in the least. Something tugged at my heart within this moment whilst my mind and body told me that I was being threatened, but no one was around.

I returned to Mary and placed a crest that had been attached to a chain around her neck. I knew it would be best to bring a religious figure into this battle that had been thrust upon us. She questioned me on what we should do as I said nothing and began to pray. Mary followed me and said a prayer of her own at this moment, but I knew that she was still hesitant. I then sat in my chair and resumed smoking my pipe as Mary stared in my direction.

"So we will do nothing about this?" She asked. I said nothing but nodded as I waited to hear the sounds of escalation within our home. The sun had begun its final phase of setting below the horizon so it was a matter of time. This time, however, I would not allow a demon to have the upper hand.

I stayed sitting in my chair on the porch for a few more moments as I continued to think about our next moves. The calm of the day began elevating itself to a fever pitch which pushed my heart to pound within my chest. The air had become thick and tense as Mary began to lose all grip upon her sanity. I was intent, however, to bring Mary into the fold and allow her to stand in for Edric. I knew that I would need help in facing this entity for the last time, but she would have to be brought to speed on the issue. I then brought the fire rod from the sitting room and placed it in her hand as I explained the importance of iron against entities.

She gazed up at me as if I were jesting but I continued with my serious tone as she slowly realized that I was not joking. It then dawned upon her mind that I was bringing her into the fight as I should have done from the beginning. A small amount of comfort washed over her as she asked me for the other fire rod from the kitchen as well. I retrieved the item for her as she laid them both across her lap in a crossed manner to form a holy cross. I could not tell if this was a natural position for her or simply something she had been guided to do, but it made sense. Mary seemed to show that she was a natural at this moment which gave me comfort as well.

Our home behind us seemed to begin knocking and thumping as though an army were moving about within the structure. Mary and I sat resolute and unflinching within our chairs just outside and waited for the sun to sink below the horizon. We both knew that this night would hold many struggles, but were determined to end this for good. I produced a bottle of holy water from my chest pocket and sprinkled her as we both prayed. She then did the same for me to bring a level of protection over each other.

I then took her hand and knelt before her to profess my love if something untoward would happen.

"My darling Mary, I love you more than life itself, and should I fall remember this until your dying breath. Do not see my sufferings as a man, but my glimmering peace as a soul at that moment. Shed not a tear for me as I would travel across the oceans and all of the time to be with you in another life." Mary shed a small tear as she accepted this and kissed me passionately while also reciprocating the sentiment.

I knew that she would never wish for me to linger upon this earth without knowing her last feeling toward me was pure love and romance. Mary made no small gesture in allowing me to know her heart within this moment as we both knew what risks were involved. This being was powerful indeed and nothing would ensure that we would both be unscathed from this fight. Though we were both confident that we would be able to return from the fray together and hold our sacred love forever. Now it was that we kissed as I held her hands upon my chest and placed my forehead upon hers. I was dedicated to this woman of grace and angelic beauty and she to me.

We both stood for the moment as she could feel the tensions growing in the air around us with the last glimmers of sunlight. It was then that we could hear the herb bushes and flowers rustling within the yard just beyond us. We turned to see a movement of the plants as though someone was stepping out of the brush and onto the grass. No form could be witnessed, but the shapes of feet stepping through the grass and then thudding across the porch behind me and into the home. I nodded to Mary as we both readied ourselves for whatever we may face within our home.

I made my way into the doorway of the home along with Mary behind me as we systematically closed all of the doors and windows on the lower lever. We locked our doors in an unusual fashion and moved to meet in the dining room. There was no indication of which direction the footsteps had moved within these walls, but it did not matter. Within the moment, we would find this being and bring our defenses bare. Then we stopped dead in our steps as feet could be heard stomping across the floor above us within the space that was an extra and unfinished room. The thudding grew louder and louder until it was directly above us; then it stopped.

I brought out my bible and opened it to revelation as I began reading random passages that seemed appropriate. Mary stood looking all about as my words echoed throughout our home and silence reigned throughout the home. I then closed the Bible as Mary and I prayed aloud together if not to give us defense, but to intimidate this entity. The last measure was to produce a silver long knife that I had purchased and my new pistol. I had to be sure that my shots would land well upon the demon and not through a window or the walls of the home. I prepared my mind for a moment until the thumping resumed and moved to the upper landing of the stairs.

Loud steps could be heard moving steadily down the stairs and around the corner as the unholy beast emerged. Its full form was appalling, to say the least, which gave to confusion as this did not seem within its realm. I looked about as the being approached only to realize that it had mustered the strength to show itself within our world. I then witnessed the being shift into that of the horrid hag which had attempted to grasp me in North Carolina. Its dead skin and hanging hair along with the rotting smell of long death upon it. I simply raised my pistol and fired into its body as the sound of the gun seemed to not ring about.

I knew now that we were isolated and alone without any help from another party who could hear such a loud sound. The shot was true and blew a chunk of flesh from the chest of this being. Curdled blood spilled about the floor as this thing stopped and grasped at the gaping hole. It was then that a shrieking sound emanated from the being enough to temporarily deafen Mary and myself. I found my bearings once more and fired the next shot into its shoulder which removed the right arm. More blood dripped down its side as the arm fell to the ground with more shrieking ringing out. It then laughed as muddled uttering emanated from the mouth along with the movement from the freshly removed arm.

It sprang forward as Mary ran it through the side which stopped its advance and I placed my knife into the spot within which the heart would be housed. Though I was not sure that the heart would be present in this abomination. This left it to stagger back for a moment then melt into a thick black goo upon the floor. This led to the emergence of my mother and aunt in a sagging horror that had been conjoined together. They were naked and disgusting looking as though corpses were raised from the dead. Their skin was greyed and tight against their bones with some innards showing through and hanging out.

So it was that they moved forward cackling as Mary and I moved to the sides and flanked them. We both placed a cloth over our noses to not smell such rot and puss. One after the other, Mary and I bludgeoned and slashed our way through the two horrors in an instant. This caused a new form to emerge from the pile of flesh as my father had begun melding from such horror.

"Stop this fighting at once Benjamin! Your mother commands it!"

His words were deeper than normal and began to distort as he wrapped his hand around my leg while trying to pull me into this pile of rot. I slashed his arm from his body while it began clamping tighter around my leg. Mary then shoved the fire rod through his skill which brought an end to this nightmare.

We found ourselves blinking and standing within an empty space once more as everything vanished into thin air. I could not understand this but it gave Mary and me the need to be at each other's backs. We turned all about and looked from top to bottom to see anything else that would meet us. It was then that a rumbling began moving underneath the home and moved toward us. Black protrusions emerged from the walls and began shooting across the hallway as Mary and I ducked under them and ran from each other. There came a loud banging noise that rang out once these forms were absorbed into the walls once more. The candles within the home began to flicker violently within their holders. Mary grasped the candle from the setting at the bottom nook beside the stairs and began moving toward me.

The rumbling began again as the form morphed and dropped from the ceiling between us. I immediately fired a shot into the body of this being as the bullet seemed to have little effect. Instead, I allowed Mary the next set of blows as she tore deep into the back of the being with the fire rods from each hand. I dropped to my knee and placed a charge at the feet of the demon and yelled for Mary to move. The being started toward me as I fired into the charge sending smoke and herbs into the air. A gargling sound emanated from the being as it toppled backward and onto the ground. I then rushed forward along with Mary and began slashing the being. Mary held nothing back as she struck the thing over and over.

This did little to stop such a being as it simply formed into a sphere and rolled from under our barrage toward the wall. I then lunged forward and was struck across my chest and thrown back toward the front door. The breath was knocked from me as I lay on the ground hearing Mary slam into the being. I stood to see her take a hit as well and fly into the rear hallway of the home. The rods had been separated from her grasp as the being began walking toward her in a rocking motion. I threw another charge in its path as I fired into the packaging which pushed the being back toward the wall.

This allowed me time to close in on the demon and press the attack once more. I slashed and stabbed whilst placing my gun back within its holster. Mary returned as well and continued to hit at the demon until and formed into a puddle and slid into the sitting room. I rushed after it as Mary collected herself once more. I moved into the room only to find an empty room of chairs and a fireplace with nothing else. I looked about the darkened room to spy anything out of place as I moved forward cautiously. It was then that shriveled hands reached out and grasped my shoulders while pulling me in. I could feel the wet and sloppy skin separating from the bones against my skin as I was being yanked into the darkness of the corner and absorbed.

I now stood in the void world as I watched Mary approach the corner. I yelled out for her to return to the hallway as I stabbed about in the dark of the area. The only thing that could be measured was the earthen stench of this place as everything was too dark to see. The only light came about as the witch began moving toward me once more. I did all that I could know to do and produced my firearm as I lined up the shot and leveled a blast into the being. I could hear the screeching again, but this time it could be felt by every fiber of my being. This place brought on any pain it could fell upon me as I would continue to fight my way further out.

I could now feel as though I had been shot multiple times as the pain grew with each shot into this entity. I then found that I had emptied my pistol completely and then brought my second gun to bear. I continued to fire as the pain and the blood showered from my body before me. The pressure and the cutting pain grew with each moment until I knelt trying to catch my breath. I looked up in defiance only to see the witch topple upon its back and fade from sight while I only began to realize that I had been returned to the sitting room. Blood no longer flowed from my body and my mind had become resolute that nothing had happened to me. This brought peace to me as I felt Mary embrace my body only to have more pain surge throughout me.

She then stood back and made sure that I was unharmed by inspecting my arms and chest. I allowed her to comfort me at this moment as I dropped my guard and succumbed to her loving and gentle touch. I felt comforted as I had never been before until this moment. Mary hugged me as I could see the demon forming behind her. I pushed her to the side as a tentacle stretched toward me and I slashed it away. The being staggered back slightly as I moved forward and plunged my blade deep within its body. My ears then began to ring with the sounds of screeching emanating from this being.

I then pulled my blade and continued to stab over and over like a murderer in a fit of rage. The milky blackness of its body felt like flesh in the moment, but I could not stop myself from continuing to stab. I had pushed the being back and into the hallway until I was thrown upon my back and into the sitting room. Mary followed by rushing in and slamming the iron rods onto the beast whilst the screeching continued. She continued this assault until I had regained my footing and grasped my blade once more. Mary then pushed away and into the wall as I hesitated to move toward the demon again.

Knowing now that I had no more shots to speak of from either of my guns, I dropped them to the ground and drew my other iron beat stick. I knew that this would cause me to close into the creature's grasp further but I could not care. Rage had begun overtaking me as I had never felt before. My vision, however, did not become diminished or impaired in any way yet a clear focus overtook me. I could see and understand more within this state as I yelled and ran forward. I thrust my blades one after the other into the being as quickly as I could. The resistance that I had once felt was no longer present as my strength had been increased tenfold.

Mary joined in with me and began running the rods she held into the body of this being until it faltered and threw us back once more. Mary collided with the wall hard enough to shake the foundation of the home as I feared that she was hurt. I ran to her and shook her for a moment until she moved to her feet again and spit a small amount of blood onto the ground. This would turn brutal as she too had been overcome with rage until she pressed the attack again. This time, however, she would push the demon back to the stairs. The demon then turned and started moving around the corner and to the top landing.

I grasped my blade firmly within my hand and began sprinting to the stairs and up them. I began rounding the turn in the structure as I heard a loud crash as though the wall had been removed.

"MAARRRYYYY!" I yelled out in a panic.

I ran to the top of the stairs to find the being sinking into the flooring until it vanished into the void again. I threw holy water upon the opening and began praying as I focused on sealing the portal for good. The air immediately lifted until I noticed the hold within the wall beyond the closing pool.

My heart sank deep into my stomach as I realized that Mary was nowhere to be found. I approached the hole and gazed down upon the immobile form of Mary laying in the street below. I yelled for her again as I leaped down to the bushes below and rushed to her side. I began sobbing immediately as I could see her lifeless and broken body laying at my feet. My chest felt as though someone had punched me firmly until I was forced to my knees. I grasped her within my arms and held her tight as I felt her last breath leave her. The tears continued to fall upon her as I hoped with all my heart that they would return life to her again. I knew that nothing could be done for her, but I cried out for help in the night.

My love had been taken at that moment as my heart fractured from the pain of losing her. My beautiful and loving wife had been lost to this demon before my very eyes as thoughts of all that I could do differently flooded my mind.

"Help Me!!! Someone!!!" I cried out.

Only a few rushed to me as I continued to hold her in my arms and rock back and forth sobbing for what felt like an eternity. Mary had left for a better realm and I had been left to my own once again. No hope could be felt within this moment as I could not let go of the form she had once inhabited.

EPILOGUE

The rain pounded upon the brick and stone streets as the cool air of the alley stirred around me. My coat and hat had been soaked from the moisture falling all around me. The only light that could be seen was that of the moon that shone into the alley. I stood in the darkness across from the church as mourners entered the building. They trudged through the rain slowly and without any hope as their faces reflected the pain and loss in their lives. I could see that Mary's family had arrived in the city without my assistance in finding any resources for Mary's burial. The whiskery had taken me for days and entrenched me within our home as I drowned the memories of her.

I could not stop the pain of seeing the light from within the church and the faint image of the coffin on display through the doorway. I knew that it would be prudent to enter the building and mourn as well, but I could not bring myself to such things through my shame. Mary was all that I had along with the promises to care for her and keep her safe which instilled a sense of shame within me. I could not look into her father and mother's eyes and mourn in the way that they would as I was not innocent. I felt the weight of her death upon my shoulders along with the sorrow from deep inside. It was all that I could do to turn and leave the other way from the alley.

AFTERWORD

Go to hangarɪpublishing.com to learn more about the Author and stay up to date with their newest releases.

www.ingramcontent.com/pod-product-compliance
Lightning Source LLC
Chambersburg PA
CBHW061158120626
46546CB00005B/2115